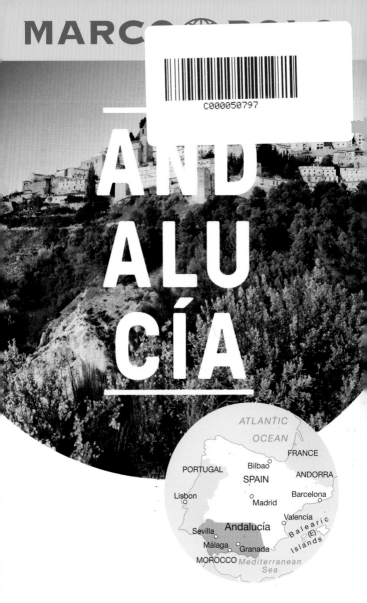

MARCO POLO

C000050797

AND
ALU
CÍA

ATLANTIC
OCEAN

FRANCE

PORTUGAL   Bilbao
SPAIN   ANDORRA

Lisbon   Barcelona
Madrid

Valencia
Andalucía   Balearic
Sevilla   (E)
Málaga   Granada   Islands

MOROCCO Mediterranean
Sea

www.marco-polo.com

FREE!

THE TOURING APP

shows you the way...
including routes and offline maps!

GET MORE OUT OF YOUR MARCO POLO GUIDE

IT'S AS SIMPLE AS THIS

1 go.marco-polo.com/and

2 download and discover

GO!

WORKS OFFLINE!

SYMBOLS

INSIDER TIP Insider Tip
★ Highlight
●●●● Best of...
☼ Scenic view
Ⓦ Responsible travel: for eco-
logical or fair trade aspects
(*) Telephone numbers that
are not toll-free

**PRICE CATEGORIES
HOTELS**

Expensive over 130 euros
Moderate 70–130 euros
Budget under 70 euros

The price for one night in a
double room for two people
without breakfast

**PRICE CATEGORIES
RESTAURANTS**

Expensive over 40 euros
Moderate 20–40 euros
Budget under 20 euros

Prices are for a three-course
menu including water or
wine

CONTENTS

DID YOU KNOW?
Timeline → p. 14
Local specialities → p. 28
For bookworms & film buffs → p. 46
The big screen in the flesh → p. 68
National holidays → p. 129
Budgeting → p. 133
Weather → p. 136

MAPS IN THE GUIDEBOOK
(144 A1) Page numbers and coordinates refer to the road atlas
(0) Site/address located off the map. Coordinates are also given for places that are not marked on the road atlas

(𝄔 A–B 2–3) Refers to the removable pull-out map

INSIDE FRONT COVER:
The best Highlights

INSIDE BACK COVER:
Maps of Córdoba, Granada, Málaga and Seville

The best MARCO POLO Insider Tips

Our top 15 Insider Tips

INSIDER TIP A train tour in an old mine

Even the Phoenicians dug for ore north of Huelva. The *Minas de Riotinto* are now a memorial to an industrial past open to the public. The visitor's park includes a historical residential neighbourhood, an old diesel train and a steam engine, both of which chug around this impressive lunar landscape → p. 126

INSIDER TIP Sand cliffs

A massive dune 100 m/328 ft high stretches across 23 km/14 mi of beach. Where? Drive to the parking lot of the *Cuesta Maneli* near Mazagón, located along the Costa de la Luz (photo above) → p. 46

INSIDER TIP Hidden beauties

Courtyards are more than just rooms without roofs – they are hubs of family life and places to gather in the open-air rolled into one. During the *Festival de los Patios* in Córdoba, an award is given to the *patio* with the most beautiful floral display (photo on opposite page) → p. 128

INSIDER TIP Hollywood days

In the outback of Cádiz, you'll find the astonishing Hotel *Utopía,* where everything is decorated in the style of the 1930s – the rooms, the restaurant and even the live entertainment → p. 82

INSIDER TIP The forgotten village

Don't tell anyone! On the Costa del Sol there is an unspoilt, little-visited village – *Maro* – bathing in the sun above the sea with its own sandy beach → p. 95

INSIDER TIP A shop like a garage sale

La Recova in Málaga is a charming restaurant and an unusual shop offering Spanish crafts and all the things stored on the shelves and in the cabinets of granny's attic → p. 89

INSIDER TIP Great tapas

Granada is the tapas capital. The *Taberna La Tana* is small, excellent and not in the least touristy. Wide choice of wines by the glass → p. 69

INSIDER TIP A trip to remember

The countryside is like a road movie set. The *Altiplano* in Granada province seems unforgiving, high and endless. Just go for a drive and be amazed → p. 114

INSIDER TIP The Orient in the West

The Moorish past is not only visible in the Alhambra and Mezquita, but also in the Jewish quarter of Córdoba in the *Capilla de San Bartolomé* → p. 37

INSIDER TIP Beach racing

The first race on the beach at Sanlúcar de Barrameda was held more than 160 years ago. Bet, have fun and be seen – the *Carreras de Caballo* has everything that a horse-race should have → p. 129

INSIDER TIP A night near the grottos

Don't just look at the caves and move on. Stay the night in Guadix at *Abentofail*, an affordable and beautiful Old Town hotel with an amazing restaurant → p. 72

INSIDER TIP Mini hotel in Marbella

How to avoid the glittery big hotels in Marbella – try *La Morada Más Hermosa*, a small *hostal* with six charming rooms and a lemon tree → p. 93

INSIDER TIP Sitting pretty

Higher up, explore the fortress, mosque and bullring; further down, stroll around the picturesque narrow streets. *Almonaster la Real* is the most beautiful place in the Sierra de Aracena → p. 35

INSIDER TIP Morning glory

Wanting a delicious and healthy breakfast? At *Hotel Misiana* in Tarifa, you'll start the day on the right track → p. 99

INSIDER TIP Barbecuing in the country

Tucked away in a shady spot not far from Vejer de la Frontera is an open-air restaurant called *La Castillería,* where Juan Valdés demonstrates his culinary and barbecue skills → p. 83

BEST OF...

FOR FREE

● **Baroque in Seville at its best**

The *Siglo de Oro*, the 'Golden Age', was a period in which the arts flourished in Spain. Master painters include Diego Velázquez, Francisco de Zurbarán and José de Ribera. The *Museo de Bellas Artes* in Seville is free if you have a passport from an EU country → p. 51

● **The Alhambra in all its glory**

Sitting at the *Mirador de San Nicolás* and soaking in the scene is one of the many delights of a visit to Granada (photo below) → p. 66

● **Roman metropolis**

A retirement home in Andalucía was something that appealed to the Romans who built *Itálica*, too. EU passport holders can wander among the ruins free of charge and marvel at the huge amphitheatre → p. 57

● **Tapas served traditionally**

With many students living in *Granada*, the tapas culture still lives on today. The server will bring you something small to eat with every drink ordered – completely free of charge! → p. 70

● **The different faces of Málaga**

Audio guides (available at the tourist information centre) take you on seven different tours around this coastal city free of charge → p. 95

● **3000 years of art and history**

At the *Museo de Cádiz*, you'll stroll through the realms of ethnology, archaeology and the fine arts. A Phoenician sarcophagus and a cycle of paintings by Francisco de Zurbarán are among the highlights → p. 78

● **Mornings in the Mezquita**

Experience Córdoba's main attraction between 8.30am and 10am on weekdays, when a service is being held (of course without disturbing it). Let the building cast its spell on you as you listen to the Catholic mass, surrounded by Islamic architecture → p. 39

●●●● Dots in guidebook refer to 'Best of...' tips

ONLY IN ANDALUCÍA
Unique experiences

● *Gripping scenes*

Watching floats weighing several tonnes being carried on people's shoulders during *Semana Santa* is moving even for those who are not religious. Seville is the main centre for the processions of penitents (photo) → p. 128

● *Jumbles of white dice*

Whitewashed houses are typical of Andalucían villages, and those perched on mountain slopes are especially picturesque. But there are few white towns as pretty as *Vejer de la Frontera* → p. 83

● *Sublime beaches*

With 320 days of sunshine, and known as *Playa del Mónsul,* the beaches of the Cabo de Gata Natural Park are simply a dream. Crystal-clear waters and fine sand overlook a volcanic landscape → p. 62

● *A sea of olive trees*

There are more than 60 million olive trees in the south of Spain – mostly in Jaén province. This rather monotonous landscape has a magic of its own that can best be experienced from up high. For example from the Plaza Santa Lucía in *Úbeda* → p. 75

● *DIY Flamenco*

Flamenco dancing is infectious, so why not learn a few steps yourself? Go for it! Try it out in Seville at the *Taller Flamenco* or at the *Fundación Cristina Heeren* → p. 54

● *Moorish legacy*

Even Christian conquerors have been known to lose their breath upon seeing the beauty of Islamic architecture. Peter the Cruel was no exception and even had his residence in Seville, the *Real Alcázar*, built in accordance to the Alhambra palace → p. 52

● *Keeping cool*

Gazpacho, the ice-cold soup for hot weather, has come a long way. The mixture of fresh tomatoes, cucumbers, peppers and dried bread was originally a dish for poorer people. Many gourmet chefs nowadays, however, have turned it into a supreme delicacy – for example, at *El Churrasco* in Córdoba or in Málaga at *José Carlos García* → p. 40, 89

ONLY IN

BEST OF...

AND IF IT RAINS?
Activities to brighten your day

● *The master of modern art*
Take time to admire the unique collection of some 200 works in the *Picasso Museum* in Málaga → p. 89

● *Bodega tours*
Many exciting *bodega tours* are offered in Jerez de la Frontera. While getting to know the city's bodegas, you'll learn about the history of Sherry wine in Andalucía → p. 84

● *Cars and paintings*
At the *Tabacalera* in Málaga, you can visit an old tobacco factory, go to an automobile exhibition and then study the paintings in the Russian Museum (photo) → p. 89

● *Count the fish and keep dry*
At the *Acuario de Sevilla*, you can safely watch sharks and octopi from behind armoured glass → p. 124

● *Tornado alarm!*
At the *Parque de las Ciencias* in Granada, you'll learn how a tornado develops, how easily the senses are deceived and how much electricity you can generate on a bicycle. Children and adults will enjoy playing, experimenting and marvelling at the results → p. 126

● *A walk on the beach*
Bolonia is a peaceful and hidden village where the clouds hang low and the wind always blows. Take a walk on the beach – but walk against the wind and rain for an unforgettable experience → p. 100

● *Flamenco at its best*
If you need a distraction from the rain or happen to be in low spirits, head down to *Tablao Cardenal* in Córdoba for a night and get lost in the passion and heat of the night → p. 41

RAIN

RELAX AND CHILL OUT
Take it easy and spoil yourself

● *Arab baths*
At *Hammam Al Ándalus* in Córdoba, the Arab baths are surrounded by dark red walls and filled with water that glows turquoise. You're sure to spoil your senses while bathing under the many domes and Moorish horseshoe arches → **p. 40**

● *Peace in the city centre*
A dip in the roof-top pool does a world of good after a shopping trip or touring the sites. Spoil yourself silly in the designer spa at the *EME Catedral* hotel – and take your evening drink up on the roof, too. The view of Seville by night is simply fantastic → **p. 56**

● *The patios of Córdoba*
Most visitors come to Córdoba to see the Mezquita and then move on. It's worth it, however, to stay at one of the city's charming hotels and see some of the magnificent patios at, for example, the *Balcón de Córdoba* or the *Casa de los Azulejos* → **p. 41**

● *Seafood as the grand menu*
At *Aponiente* in El Puerto de Santa María, you can order an 18-course meal called 'Far al Fondo' and take your senses on a Mediterranean journey. This palatable masterpiece of new, Andalucían cuisine is by Ángel León, an ambitious top chef, and is all yours for just 205 euros. Too expensive? Well, rare experiences do have a price → **p. 86**

● *A patio with patina*
With its many palaces and churches, Carmona is much calmer than Seville and Córdoba. Spend the night at the *Parador de Carmona,* one of Spain's most beautiful hotels. It's built over a 14th-century Moorish fortress and features a courtyard with fountains where you can forget about the time → **p. 57**

● *Rest awhile*
When Seville gets tiring, take a siesta in the *Parque de María Luisa*. This former site of the 1929 Ibero-American Exposition is now a landscaped park with water features and greenery. The benches on the *Plaza de España* are ideal for reading – sit back and relax! (photo) → **p. 52**

DISCOVER ANDALUCÍA!

When we think of Spain, we see the sun and seaside, bullfights and flamenco, proud people and Moorish splendour. This is Andalucía! The place where Europe comes closest to Africa. The *Arab culture* shaped this region for almost 800 years, leaving behind treasures like the Alhambra in Granada and the Mezquita in Córdoba. With southern Spain being such a diverse travel destination, you'll find everything from sand to snow, solitude to excitement, and opulent luxury to simple southern living.

The *pueblos blancos* are simply fascinating. These white villages are filled with serene courtyards and tight alleyways that twist and turn and even incline at times. Lemons, oranges and olives grow on the trees planted majestically before ancient walls. Age-old fortresses are built atop rugged cliffs, and magnificent *churches and cathedrals* chronicle a history shared by both Islam and Christianity. You'll find *plenty of beaches, sun and seaside*, and the sporting activites are neverending. Whether you're looking to ride horseback, climb, kitesurf or golf, your wishes will be fully met. For hiking and cycling activities, the most beloved areas are in the Sierra Nevada, in the forests of the Sierra de Aracena and throughout the Cazorla Nature Park.

Belongs on the bucket list: the beaches on Cabo de Gata, e.g. the Playa del Arco

While exploring, it's common to find vultures, eagles and other animals in the southern mountain range.

To understand what makes the *Andalucían culture and lifestyle* so unique, it's best to look at their history. Led by Tariq Ibn Ziyad, the Moors crossed the Strait of Gibraltar in 711. In just eight years, these North African conquerors claimed almost all of the Iberian Peninsula, making Andalucía the most Islamic-influenced region in Spain today. Two prime examples are the *Alhambra* in Granada and the *Mezquita* of Córdoba. The Alhambra symbolises the rise and fall of Arab rule in Western Europe, while the enormous Mezquita represents the mosque that once illuminated the former Caliphate of Córdoba. In Seville, you'll find Mudéjar decoration on the Plaza de

1100 BC
The Phoenicians found the city of Cádiz

206 BC
Beginning of Roman rule

409 AD
The Visigoths advance across the Iberian Peninsula

from 711
Arabic conquest of the Iberian Peninsula

8th–11th centuries
The peak of economic and cultural society under Islamic rule

mid-11th–15th centuries
Small Islamic principalities form. The Reconquista begins, and Christian armies advance as far as

España. The ornamental use of brick and coloured tiles is astonishing and remained popular well into the 20th century. But history isn't always that easy to recognise. The *Giralda*, for example, wasn't always a belltower on the Cathedral of Seville, but a minaret. Some speculate that these and other Islamic influences are the reasons for the century-old debate on religion in society and politics.

During the Franco dictatorship, political power shifted into the hands of the church, establishing a controversial Catholic state in Spain. Even today, society remains divided on the issue of church and state. Nonetheless, church celebrations are still held each year, for example, during the Holy Week of *Semana Santa*. Although the processions are well-attended, Andalucía is a much more secular and multicultural region than you might think. In the tourism industry, Andalucían's Islamic past has been used to falsely depict the region as some magical walk through the folk tales described in *Arabian Nights*. In reality, however, the country has many other cultural influences, as many Latin Americans, Eastern Europeans and North Africans immigrated to Spain in the 1990s.

Nonetheless, as the number of Muslims living here grows, the Islamic culture is becoming more present in the region. This can be seen, for example, in the *tearooms and souvenir shops* in Granada where Moroccan handicrafts are sold, as well as in the Moorish district of Albaicín, where Andalucía's first modern mosque has

> **Traces of an 800-year-old Arab culture**

Andalucía. The entire region, apart from the Kingdom of Granada, falls to the Kingdom of Castile

1492
Isabella of Castile and Ferdinand of Aragón capture Granada. Expulsion of Jews and Muslims. Columbus discovers America

1516
Charles V becomes the first ruler of the Habsburg dynasty in Spain

1714
The Bourbons ascend the Spanish throne. Gibraltar becomes British

1808–14
The Peninsular War against Napoleon

been built. Such developments, however, have been met with tension – not surprising considering the country's culture was defined during the Reconquista, consisting of eight centuries of Christian reconquest. On the one hand, Muslims have been denied permission to hold Friday prayers in the Mezquita of Córdoba. On the other hand, religious radicals have called for all Muslims to recounquer al-Andalus for themselves.

> **An exciting city life has established itself in the metropolitan areas**

The region's history, however, isn't only religion-based. In cities like Granada and Málaga, the culture is evolving. Especially in the region's capital of Seville, an *exciting city life* has been established, and a new cultural era is being celebrated, similar to the ones in Madrid (1980s) and Barcelona (1990s). Everywhere you turn, you see modern fashion shops, *trendy bars and hip restaurants*. Yet despite these changes, religious traditions like the Feria de abril, Catholic brotherhoods and Marian devotions have remained. It is the very co-existence of these eras and perspectives that make Andalucía so fascinating.

Central Europeans' fascination with Andalucía began in the 19th century, when *flamenco music* was on the rise and the *gitanos'* culture (the Romani people in Spain) was popular. This facination grew even further in the 1960s with mass tourism. Although some of the cliches you may have heard about Andalucía are true, they don't define the culture. Some are seen in everyday life, while others are only celebrated on national holidays.

Not everything is ancient and intriguing here, however. Spain's culture also has its cruel side, but things are slowly improving. The ethics of *bullfighting* are currently being dedated in Corrida, the city it originates from. It remains uncertain if it will be banned or, like the Mediterranean diet or flamenco, protected as part of the country's cultural heritage. Time will tell. Unlike bullfighting, flamenco is gaining popularity and developing itself in places beyond the *tablaos* where tourists go to experience this art form. The music's *Arab-inspired melodies and complex rhythms* are even starting to influence contemporary pop music. In an area the size of Portugal, Andalucía is obviously no longer behind the times. You can rest assured that the 8.4 million people living here are very much a part of 21st-century Europe.

1936–39	1975	1981	2008–14	2017
Spanish Civil War – The Republicans are defeated and General Francisco Franco establishes a dictatorship	Franco dies. Juan Carlos I is crowned king and a transition to democracy is made	Andalucia becomes autonomous with its own regional government	The housing slump and the global economic crisis cripple Andalucia	Andalucia draws a record-breaking number of tourists for the third year in a row

The colourful Centre Pompidou Málaga: a museum both modern and hip

To paint an accurate picture of the region's landscape, it requires a bit more than a romantic description of *olive trees* growing before ancient walls. The olive tree plantations that monotonously spread forever across northeast Andalucía are also a part of the scenery. Moorish palaces and charming white villages are only one side of the coin. On the other are bleak and repetitive apartment blocks and coastal cottage settlements that cover more than two-thirds of the

A kaleidascope of landscapes and a feast for the senses

Mediterranean coastline. Economically speaking, Spain was fortunate to experience a housing boom at the beginning of the 21st century. Although jobs and economic growth were created, illegal land development and a loss of natural habitat also followed. Fortunately, the coast is now protected by legislation. The region has also seen some positive developments in conservation, including the expansion of *renewable energies*. Two prime examples are the solar panels covering the plateaus in La Calahorra and the countless windmills installed in the Strait of Gibraltar.

Andalucía is a *kaleidascope of landscapes*. You'll discover dunes along the Atlantic, holm oak and cork forests in the northwest, mountain ranges in the Sierra de Grazalema, semi-deserts in Almería and olive tree plantations in Jaén. In short, southern Spain is a feast for the senses. *¡Bienvenido a Andalucía!*

17

WHAT'S HOT

1 Adiós Mainstream

Om or Allah   Since the 1960s and 70s, Andalucía has been a refuge for downshifters who dream of living in the warm south, free to do whatever they please. Many of these dreamers still come to Alpujarras. Here, you'll find not only Spain's oldest community, but also the town of Órgiva, where people from over 60 nations have immigrated. At the teahouse *Baraka (C/ Estación 12 | www.teteria-baraka.com)*, you'll come across Spanish Sufis eating Halal and searching for enlightenment. This is even odd for the Monks and guests in the nearby Buddhist retreat centre *O sel Ling* (photo).

2 Flamenco Fashion

A skirt and flounce   Fashion labels like *Aldebarán* in Córdoba exhibit how exciting and trendy flamenco fashion can be. The Seville brand *Valeria Derbais* makes feminine and sensual garments using fabics like silk, satin, tulle and organza. The youth streetwear created by *Juana Martín* in Córdoba is currently all the rage. The biggest event in the fashion scene takes place in Seville: the *International Flamenco Fashion Show (Palacio de Exposiciones y Congresos | Av. Alcalde Luis Uruñuela 1)*.

3 The Joy of Cycling

Calm or action-packed   It wasn't that long ago when bikes were a hot commodity in Andalucía. Today, both young and old can be seen cycling through the city of Seville on trendy rental bikes (photo). At weekends, fathers ride along the Costa del Sol on their road bikes. And where the trail isn't paved, there's a dirt one nearby. In the nature parks, Andalucíans, sweat and adrenalin fueled, enjoy riding their *Bicicleta Todo Terreno* (BTT) through their wild homeland!

The Sangría Revival

4

Make way for sangría The famous vermouth bars in Madrid and Barcelona have become a staple in the city nightlife, but sangría is coming back in style. This refreshing and traditional drink is best savoured in a glass, not guzzled down in some oversized bucket. Connoisseurs are looking for innovative and creative mixes. The core ingredient is usually red wine, but who's to say you can't use cointreau, champagne, brandy, vermouth, lemon juice, oranges, strawberries or wild berries? Offering ready-mixed drinks, stores like *Lolea* and *La Tita Rivera* are jumping on the bandwagon, but any experienced barkeeper will tell you homemade is best!

Nobel Craftwork

5

Luxurious living Hand-painted ceramics, intricate inlays and embroidery; forging and wickerwork. The artisans in Andalucía are many and skilled, but can they sustain a living this way? Their hope is that tourists buy something to take back home with them, but there's never a guarantee. As a result, some artisans have turned their focus to the upper class. *Paco Luis Martos (artesonados.es),* for example, creates highly-complex coffered ceilings in Mudéjar style in his workshop in Úbeda. Martos has been contracted not only to restore old palaces, but also by the super rich in the US Gulf States, where his art is cherished. *Pielfort (pielfort.es)* also offers luxury items. Why have a luxury label like Dior craft your bag when you can have it personalised in Ubrique, the leather capital of the world? The idea seems to be taking off. Today, Pielfort is being worn by people in the royal houses and dynasties of Morocco and Monaco, and the label even managed to land a spot in Monocle Magazine.

IN A NUTSHELL

WHITE OR BLUE?

Nearly all the towns and villages in Andalucía are painted white. Considered a job for the housewife, whitewashing first became a thing in the 17th century. But to be a tourist attraction, a *pueblo blanco* has to offer a bit more than simply a town of whitewashed buildings. They also have to provide tourists with narrow alleyways where they can easily get lost! Only then can a town or village be of Moorish origin. And for picture taking, it doesn't hurt to have the village beautifully placed on a hillside or on a rocky cliff somewhere. The most beautiful *pueblos blancos* can be found in Vejer de la Frontera, Arcos de la Frontera, Grazalema, Gaucín, Comares, Casares and Frigiliana. There is one village, however, that stands out from the rest, called Júzcar. Located between Ronda and Estepona, this village has been painted sky-blue. It started as a pomotional gag by Sony Pictures and required 9000 buckets of light-blue paint – the perfect backdrop for the premiere of the 'Smurfs' movie. Although that was some years ago, after thousands of visitors started coming to see the *pueblo azul*, nobody in the village wanted their whitewashed houses back.

CHAINS & CAPRIOTES

Semana Santa marks the Holy Week in Spain and is best seen in Seville, where over 50 Catholic brotherhoods *(cofradías or hermandades)* hold processions in Andalucía. During these celebrations, figures of the crucified Christ and Virgin

How a billboard became part of cultural heritage. Who grooms the Andalucían landscape? Have the Smurfs moved to Spain?

Mary are placed on *pasos* (EN: floats) and surrounded by a sea of candles. The *pasos,* which can weigh up to several tonnes, are mournfully carried through the city's alleys by *costaleros*. These barefooted penitents march with shackels around their ankles and wear capirotes to hide their faces. In the 14th century during the Black Death in Málaga, the city lost many of their strong men. Needing people to carry the *pasos,* they turned to the town jail for help. Today, this is tradition in Málaga. Each year, one prison-

er is chosen to carry the *paso* through Seville, and, in doing so, their sentence is forever pardoned.

KEEP CALM AND DANCE

The music to a sad song slowly builds on stage. Sitting quietly and upright in her chair, the singer appears in a trance-like state. Suddenly, a drawn out *aayyyy* escapes her lips: the famous 'cry of pain' in flamenco music. She seems to be singing about an unfaithful lover or her deceased brother. The song represents one of 40-odd styles of flamenco music. She starts with the melancholic *siguiriya* and then presents the famous *fandango*. Although her voice isn't perfect, the audience still enjoys the performance. The music is more about how powerful one can express *jondura*, or emotional depth. The audience yells *¡Olé!* to cheer her on. Accompanying her singing, she begins clapping a complex rhythm, a style of clapping known as *palmas*. The flamenco she's presenting has its beginnings in the second half of the 18th century in Jerez de la Fronteraof Cádiz and Triana of Seville. The genre has its roots in Romani music and Andalucían folk. Flamenco became most popular between 1860 and 1910. Nonetheless, people still enjoy watching the dance performance among a large audience, and flamenco guitar-playing is a widespread artform. With most *flamencos* (EN: flamenco artists) being Romani, many believe that a *payo*, a non-Romani, is unable to reach the Romas' level of artistry. When attending a concert at one of the many *tablaos*, you'll find the songs and dance to be lively and cheerful. What you probably won't see, however, is the *duende*: the soul of flamenco music. This spirit magically channels the emotions created by the artist and sends them into the audience. For more information, visit *www.andalucia.org/flamenco*

L AND AHOY!

Palos de la Frontera is a unique place. On the outside, it's just another small, whitewashed town near Huelva, but its connection to Christopher Columbus is what makes it special. Here's where Columbus set sail to discover the New World. Known as Cristóbal Colón in Spanish, he was one of the crazies in the 15th century who claimed the earth was

actually round. On 3 August 1492, he bravely headed west in hopes of finding a route to India in the east. Although Columbus spotted land on 12 October, he and his crew were unaware that they were the first Europeans to discover America; a discovery that would later make Spain the largest global empire of the 16th century. Although he was successful, Palos de la Frontera was an unusual starting point, considering that there's no seaside here and the river's miles away. He started in the mouth of the Río Tinto and sailed into the Río Odiel. While visiting the town today, you'll find paintings of caravels on the buildings and a monument in the square that captures the spirit of adventure on the open sea. Under the San Jorge Church, you'll find the well that Columbus used to supply his three legendary ships with water: the Niña, the Pinta and the Santa María. Although the harbour has long since become silted, it's still possible to trace Columbus' steps here. Replicas of his three ships, for example, are on display at a delightful museum called the 'Wharf of the Caravels', where Columbus began his journey. No matter your age, you're sure to enjoy climbing on the decks and pretending to be one of the greatest and most well-renowned sailors of all time.

T WO LORRIES OF ART

Born in Málaga, Pablo Ruiz Picasso (1881–1973), a brilliant 20th-century artist, only spent a few years of his childhood here. In 1891, after his father, an art teacher, was offered a job in La Coruña, the family moved to Galicia and then to Barcelona a few years later. After the Spanish Civil War, with dictator Franco still in power, Picasso refused to set foot in his home country. Wanting, however, to present his art there, in 1953, Picasso had two lorry loads of his paintings sent to the Palacio de Buenavista in Málaga. The Franco regime, however, forbade the display of his art. Fifty years later, the same palace now houses the Museo Picasso Málaga, where 155 works are now the centrepiece of the museum – a gift from Christine Ruiz-Picasso, the widow of Paolo, Picasso's first son.

BORN TO FLAMENCO

It's uncertain how many Romas, or *gitanos* (Romani people in Spain), live in the country. Statistics say somewhere between 650,000 and 700,000; nearly 2% of the population. Some 300,000 Romas live in Andalucía, where they first settled in the 15th century. They remain, however, a segregated people not interested in integrating. They prefer to preserve their cultural autonomy. Consequently, *gitanos* and *payos* (non-Romas) live side by side, completely clueless of each other's culture and lifestyle. Although the Romas have contributed greatly to the culture by bringing flamenco music to Spain, studies indicate they are the most rejected minority in the country. Society critisises the high infant-mortality rate, the low life expectancy and the school dropout rate among the Romas. To ease tensions, the Secretariado Gitano Foundation works to get Romas qualified and integrated into society while still 'promoting the recognition of the cultural identity of the Roma community', a challenge that requires all of society to change.

CUE THE SUN!

On the plateaus near La Calahorra where the opening scene of 'Once Upon a Time in the West' was shot, this desert landscape was once the backdrop to the

Flamenco – breathtaking moves, magical vibes and the cry of *aaayyy*

When the gods play tangram: olive trees form massive shapes in the province of Jaén

Wild West. Today, due to a new energy policy, it's used to generate solar electricity over an area the size of 210 football fields. The German Aerospace Center chose this location and also invented the parabolic trough collectors constructed here. Producing 150 MW, Andasol is one of the largest solar power stations in the world and is made up of three power plants: Andasol 1, 2 and 3. Unlike photovoltaic plants, solar power plants are able to produce electricity at night, which, unfortunately, requires a lot of water. If you're looking to see something incredible, visit the concentrated solar power plants in west Seville. Named PS 10 and PS 20, each plant uses 1255 mirrors to concentrate the sun's rays into a tower 100 m/328 ft high. When dust falls over the reflected sunrays, a tipi of light materialises in the sky. It's quite the spectable for any true sci-fi fan.

RICH TIMES & FINE ART

The 'Spanish Golden Age', or the *Siglo de Oro*, began after heavily-laden caravels coming from the New World docked in the ports of Seville and Cádiz. With it also came a prosperous age of flourishing art during the 17th century. Francisco Pacheco (1564–1654) opened the art school in Seville where the great master of Spanish Baroque Diego Velázquez (1599–1660) studied. Bartolomé Murillo (1618–82) and the famous monk painter Francisco de Zurbarán (1598–1664) also found work in Seville during this time. In addition, expressive, life-like sculptures of the crucified Chirst and the Virgin Mary started to emerged from this time and were carried in the Semana Santa processions. Some of these great sculptors included Pedro de Mena, Juan de Mesa, Pedro Roldán and Juan Martínez Montañés.

A CULTURE OF DEATH?

The aficionados of bullfighting are still uncertain if their beloved sport is safe from ever becoming banned as the protests against animal cruelty gain more and more momentum. But it's not only the animal protection organisations and the Catalan nationalists raising their fists these days; almost everyone in society agrees that a culture of death simply doesn't belong in Spanish society anymore. Regardless, the abolishment of bullfighting in the south of Spain is not expected to happen anytime soon. Those who want to save the sport are pushing for bullfighting to be protected as a part of Spain's cultural heritage. Suggestions are being made to make the sport more politically correct by changing the rules outlined in the *tauromaquia* (a word referring not only to the *corrida*, the bullfight, but also to the energy surrounding the sport). One of the added rules could be to make it illegal for bullfighters to slice off the bull's ears and present them like trophies to the crowd. Or they could somehow make the sport less bloody. Either way, since the rules were first written in the city of Ronda, Andalucía feels it is their duty to modify the *tauromaquia*. No one, however, dares attach their name to this highly controversial text. In the meantime, the arenas, cooks and breeders hope nothing will prevent them from serving *criadilla* (EN: bull testicles) to the fans after the bullfight.

THE BULL AHEAD

When driving through the country, you may see the silhouette of a massive bull in the distance. It's hard to miss since it's 12 m/40 ft high. The bull was made in 1957 and was initially a billboard for Osborne, the Sherry and brandy manufacturer in El Puerto de Santa María. Since then, this bull has evolved into something so much more. Today, it's seen as a symbol of Spain. How, you ask? Well, a law was passed in 1989 making it illegal for billboards to be placed on country roads. Following legislation, Osborne removed the writing from their ad but left the bull standing. In response, in 1994, the company was charged a steep fine. In response, thousands of protesters demanded that the parliament make the Osbore bull a part of Spain's cultural heritage. Surprisingly enough, they won. But the bull didn't stop there. Today, you'll also find a giant donkey on the A 4 between Bailén and Córdoba. Titled the *Burro de Cataluña* and created by two young Catalans in 2004, this billboard began as a bumper sticker to protest against the Osborne bull's fame. Today, the silhouetted donkey symbolises the Catalan people's fight for independence.

OF EPIC PROPORTION

You've got to see this! For the best view, go to the castle in Jaén or the one in Baños de la Encina – really any mountain in the Jaén province will do. From here, you'll see an endless sea of olive trees growing in rows at an equal distance from each other. But how? The olive farmers planted the trees using an underground irrigation system that beautifully groomed the landscape with magnificent shapes of epic proportion. Did you know Spain is the largest producer of olive oil in the world? Around 66 million trees are grown in the Jaén province, producing almost half of the world's olive oil! Another fun fact: there are 260 different kinds of olives, so you may need an expert to tell them apart. And in October each year, thousands of seasonal workers from Spain, Romania, Bulgaria and other countries come here to shake the olives from the trees. Does anyone need a job?

FOOD & DRINK

Well, if that doesn't wake you up! The new day in Andalucía is welcomed in with a cup of blacker-than-black coffee that even with lots of hot milk turns merely a dark brown. And this is often only accompanied by a *bollo*, a sweet bun. Breakfast must have been invented in another corner of the world.

Spanish coffee, prepared rather like an Italian espresso, is praised by aficionados – but that might not be much consolation. However, a more *typical breakfast* includes a *tostada*, a toasted slice of white bread eaten with butter and jam, olive oil and salt or oil, salt and tomato purée. The Spanish variation of the fine French croissant looks the same but has the name *cruasán*. These delicious baked goods are served with thick a layer of sticky icing on top, so you're probably better off eating it with a knife and fork. At around 11am, the Andalucíans leave their offices for a *second breakfast*. It may be rather like the first in principle, but some people order a small glass of beer and a *tapa*, a little savoury snack. In many Andalucían bars, which are generally a cross between a bar and a cafeteria, a *free tapa* is served with every soft drink or alcoholic beverage ordered. If you want to order more, simply point to whatever strikes your fancy behind the glass display cabinet and ask for *una tapa de eso* – 'one of these'. What bars and restaurants offer as tapas (*tapa* is a description of quantity, not a type of food) can also be ordered as a *ración* (a large portion). A *ración* is perfect when sharing. If

A tapas bar, gourmet temple or a pub? Wherever you decide to go, you can expect a culinary treat

you are eating alone, you probably won't need to order more than a half portion (*media ración*). If you get hungry from all the swimming you've done, head over to the next *chiringuito*, a *beach snackbar* that serves tapas and *raciónes*. Keep in mind that *lunch* in Andalucía doesn't start until 2pm and only lasts until at 4.30pm. The restaurants offer meals during lunch hours that are called *menú del día* in Spanish. The prices of these meals start at 10 euros. For each meal, you normally have a choice between three start-

ers (*primero*) *and* three main courses (*segundo*). Included with the meal are usually a pudding and a glass of table wine. When looking for the best restaurant, try to look for the place where most of the locals go; the more locals you see sitting at the tables, the better the place most likely is. When going out for *supper*, remember that Andalucíans typically eat around 9pm at the earliest and they generally eat ever later in summer. At weekends in Seville, you could well go to a restaurant at 10pm and be the only

LOCAL SPECIALITIES

ajoblanco – cold garlic soup with crushed almonds and grapes

albóndigas – meatballs

bacalao – salted and dried cod

boquerones fritos/en vinagre – anchovies, fried or in vinegar

café solo/cortado/con leche – espresso/espresso with a little milk/white coffee

calamares – squid

chipirones – baby squid

chorizo – salami with red peppers

churros – fried doughnuts (served at breakfast and commonly dipped into warm, thick and creamy chocolate: con chocolate)

clara – beer with *gaseosa* (a Spanish shandy)

ensaladilla (rusa) – Spanish potato salad in a mayonnaise dressing and mixed with vegetables (e.g. peas, carrots and asparagus)

gambas al ajillo – prawns in a heavy garlic oil

gaseosa – lemonade

gazpacho – cold vegetable soup made with tomato purée, cucumber, peppers, oil and vinegar (photo left)

horchata – refreshing, bitter drink made of tigernuts

jamón – dry cured serrano ham; the best comes from Jabugo in the Sierra de Aracena and Trevélez in the Alpujarras

mejillones – mussels

pescaítos – little fried fish

pimientos (asados) – (fried) bell peppers

pulpo – octopus

salmorejo – similar to gazpacho, but with diced eggs and bits of ham

tortilla – a Spanish omelett made with potatos. At tapa places, it's called *un pincho de tortilla* or 'a slice of tortilla' (photo right)

guests for an hour before the place suddenly fills up. The Andalucían cuisine is as varied as the region itself. *Fish and seafood* can be found everywhere close to the sea. *Gambas* and *langostinos* from Sanlúcar de Barrameda, as well as tuna (*atún*), are well known throughout Spain.

The fact that the traditional way of cooking is relatively simple does not have a negative effect on its quality. Tomatoes, peppers and garlic are almost always present. Main courses are normally served without side dishes. A little bit of salad, a few large potato wedges and that's it. The dishes gain their special flavour from the large amounts of *olive oil* used to cook the food – the only oil Spaniards cook with. Olive oil is the basis of the 'Mediterranean diet' that nutritionists consider the secret to Spaniards' longevity.

Apart from simple, down-to-earth dishes, there is a world of *refined delicacies*, too. Famous chefs from Catalonia and the Basque Country have revolutionised the art of haute cuisine (*alta cocina*) in Spain. A younger generation of dedicated chefs is following in their footsteps in Andalucía, too. They 'deconstruct' what's commonly known and whisk things into aromatic froths, conjure up hot and cold layered creations and turn regional and exotic recipes into new delights to tickle the palate.

The ultimate *jamón ibérico* comes from the northwest of Andalucía, and gourmets consider it to be the best ham in the world. Keep an eye out for the additional wording *de bellota*, meaning that the ham is from free-range ibérico pigs that have gorged themselves on acorns. What are also really scrumptious are the biscuits and baked goods. They are made with almonds, anise and olive oil, and, just like in earlier centuries, they can still be bought in some of the monasteries.

Andalucía's most famous alcoholic beverage is the *vivo de Jerez,* which is more commonly known as *Sherry* everywhere else in the world. It is a potent, fortified wine grown on chalky soil in the Sherry triangle between Jerez de la Frontera, El Puerto de Santa María and Sanlúcar de Barrameda. The barrels of Sherry are stacked up in rows of three or four barrels high and stored in *bodegas above ground*. The youngest Sherry is at the top and the oldest is at the bottom. The Sherry meant to be sold is taken from the bottom row. The barrels are then filled with the wine from the row above, which blends

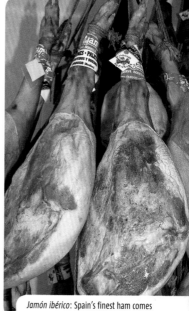

Jamón ibérico: Spain's finest ham comes from Jabugo in the Sierra de Aracena

with the older wine below. This process is repeated until the barrels at the top need to be filled with new wine. Referred to as the *solera* system, this method ensures that the taste remains the same. Vintage Sherry, therefore, does not exist.

The most famous styles of Sherry are the dry *fino* and *manzanilla* from El Puerto de Santa María and Sanlúcar de Barrameda. Both wines should be served chilled. *Amontillado*, *oloroso* and *palo cortado* sherries are softer wines. *Cream* and *pedro ximénez* are sweet and heavy. *Excellent brandy* is also matured in Sherry barrels. Unlike Sherry, 'the older the better' holds true when it comes to brandy. The wines that taste similar to Sherry come from the regions Málaga and Montilla-Moriles. Anisette is also distilled in many towns and cities throughout Andalucía.

SHOPPING

If you're wanting to take something home from Andalucía with you, you'll have many hand-crafted souvenirs to choose from, and the ceramics are particularly popular. Shop owners are allowed to be open from Monday to Saturday for 12 hours a day. Shopping on Sunday is only permitted eight times a year. With the siesta being something sacred in Spain, most shops open at 10 or 11am and close at 1.30pm. They open again in the evening from 5pm–8.30pm.

CERAMICS

Simple shapes with elaborate patterns prevail, mostly with plant-like motifs painted in bold brushstrokes in blues, yellows and greens. At first glance these may seem a little rustic and kitschy, but there's no escaping their charm. Perhaps not so pretty but very practical are *cuencos* – dishes and bowls. *Azulejos*, tiles with geometrical or plant patterns generally inspired by the Moorish tradition, are also extremely popular.

CUISINE

Andalucían specialities to be drunk or eaten are also popular souvenirs. As with wine, good olive oil depends on where it comes from. Go for the 'extra native olive oil' (*aceite de oliva virgen extra*). The fact that olive oil from different DOs (*denominación de origen*) varies in smell, colour and taste is generally due to the different olives harvested (there are more than 260 varieties). Assistants in specialist shops such as the *Casa de Aceite,* located in Baeza and in Úbeda, will be happy to advise you. The best ham in Spain is called *jamón ibérico de bellota* and comes from Jabugo. The dry-cured haunches come from a breed of pig that is only found in Spain and is traditionally fed on acorns. A good serrano ham comes from Trevélez where it is dried in the cool mountain air of the Alpujarras.

HANDICRAFTS

Leather goods artistically decorated with silver paint are a speciality of Córdoba in particular. Granada is famous for its marquetry. There is a huge selection of items from boxes of all sizes to chessboards. Less exclusive but very practical are blankets from Grazalema and unusual *jarapas* (rugs) from Frigiliana or the Alpujarras.

Hand-crafted items, affordable fashions and the coolest trends: a shopping tour in Andalucía always makes for a good time

SHERRY

Sherry, Andalucía's most famous wine, is made in Jerrez, El Puerto de Santa María and Sanlúcar de Barrameda. Consider taking a bodega tour to find the Sherry of your liking. The *fino* or *manzanilla* is dry and refreshing, but the latter is only made in Sanlúcar de Barrameda. The amber-coloured *amontillado*, with its spicy and nutty aroma, goes great with meat and cheese tapas. Needing a Sherry to go with dessert? Order the dark and sweet *oloroso* or *pedro ximénez*. If you're looking for a stronger drink, most of the bodegas produce their own brandy, too. Remember that the longer the brandy has matured, the better it will taste. In other words, unlike Sherry, 'the older the better' holds true with this drink.

SHOES & CLOTHES

If you're looking for good leather articles, Ubrique in the Sierra de Grazalema is a great place to look. But if you need riding boots, Valverde del Camino in the Huelva province is your best bet. The shoes and clothes in Andalucía are generally quite affordable. Popular fashion outlets like Zara and Mango can be found in larger cities and towns. But if you're going after the latest trends, Seville is known for its many small yet exquisite boutiques and is also the home of Andalucía's most famous fashion designer, *Victorio & Lucchino (C/ Sierpes 87)*.

SILVER

If you fancy something more upmarket, Córdoba is definitely the place to be to find stunning pieces of silver work. Here in the jewler's capital city of Andalucía, a special tradition called *filigrana cordobesa* is practiced in which gold and silver thread is formed into fine, transparent-looking pieces of jewlery. Not your style? You'll also find a wide variety of kitsch for grandma's famous display cabinet.

THE WEST

The Guadalquivir River is Andalucía's main water source. It flows westwards through Córdoba, the old caliphate city, and the capital of Seville – the heart of Andalucía. From the Doñana National Park, it flows into the Atlantic Ocean.

Córdoba has a lot more to offer than its impressive Mezquita, a 1000-year-old mosque-cathedral. And Andalucía' capital city of Seville is a city that needs to be fully experienced. After you have soaked in the magic of the Reales Alcázares and the cathedral, immerse yourself in the city's nightlife. In the neighbouring province of Huelva, the long beaches on the western Costa de la Luz, the Doñana National Park and the little-visited Sierra de Aracena are all inviting destinations.

ARACENA

(144 C2) *(∅ C3)* **Experience the feeling of going out after a rain shower on a hot summer's day by taking a walk through the many peaceful villages of Aracena. You'll breathe in the scent of green forests and walk along cool meadows shaded by chestnut trees, olive trees, cork oaks and holm oaks.**

Sevillians have long since discovered the forested hills in the Natural Park ★ *Sierra de Aracena y Picos de Aroche (www.sierradearacena.com)* to escape the seering heat of the city for a few days of relaxation. Now others are starting to explore this lovely stretch of countryside in a forgotten corner of Andalucía. The little

Lively cities and the great green outdoors: experience the best of both worlds and feel what it's like to enjoy life to the fullest

town of *Aracena* with a population of 8000 is the geographical and tourist centre of the park. You'll be sure to spend a few relaxing days in this hill town. If you are here in autumn during the mushroom and hunting season, the food will be unbelieveably delicious. In the spring, everything will be in bloom. Either way, the evenings are best spent with the locals. You'll find them in the bars of the Gran Vía or along the Plaza del Marqués. The casino, which was built in 1910 after the Andalucía art deco style, is sure to

catch your eye. The town hall and great *Parroquía de la Asunción* are also quite impressive and represent two beautiful examples of Renaissance architecture. On the ☆ hill above the town, you'll also find the ruins of a Portuguese castle that keeps watch over the people below.

SIGHTSEEING

GRUTA DE LAS MARAVILLAS
In Aracena, you can either climb or enter its hill! With a tunnel 1.2 km/0.7 mi long,

this incredible stalactite cave is a world of wonder. *Daily 10am–1.30pm and 3pm–6pm | admission 8.50 euros | C/ Pozo de la Nieve | bookings tel. 6 63 93 78 76*

JESÚS CARRIÓN

This restaurant is a favourite among locals and ranks high on many travel websites. No surprise really – the tapas are

No wonder the taste of *jamón* is so divine; the *ibérico* pigs roam free here in the Sierra de Aracena

MUSEO DEL JAMÓN

This ham museum on the green landscaped plaza of Doña Elvira isn't dedicated to just any kind of ham. Only Iberian ham takes the spotlight here, made from the *Pata Negra* pig. *Daily 10.45am–2.30pm and 3.45pm–7pm | admission 3.50 euros | Gran Vía*

FOOD & DRINK

LA DESPENSA DE JOSÉ VICENTE

This traditional restaurant in Aracena is known for serving flavoursome, local cuisine, meaning cured *ibérico* ham, fresh vegetables and mushrooms regionally picked from the area. *Closed Tue (reservations are essential in the evening) | Av. Andalucía 53 | tel. 9 59 12 84 55 | Moderate–Expensive*

outstanding, well-prepared and not at all expensive. *Closed Mon/Tue | C/ Pozo de la Nieve 35 | tel. 6 16 99 03 09 | www.jesuscarrionrestaurante.com | Moderate*

MONTECRUZ

Here, you'll find tasty tapas and local cuisine. Game specialities are served during the hunting season (Oct–Dec). *Closed Mon (except in Aug) | Plaza San Pedro | tel. 9 59 12 60 13 | Moderate–Expensive*

SPORT & LEISURE

Great hiking trails can be found all over Aracena and are most enjoyable in spring. The downside is that they aren't well marked, that is, if they 're marked at all. So do pick up a good map at the tourist information point or in the natural park's Centro de Interpretación. If you're wanting to explore the region by bike, be sure to only get your information from the Spanish website called *Las 3 Cabras* *(las3cabras.com)*.

WHERE TO STAY

INSIDER TIP CONVENTO ARACENA

Into the 1970s, the walls to this hotel were those of a convent that housed a religious community. In 2014, it became a luxurious city hotel, it and now features a beautiful spa and peaceful library located where the nave of the old church used to be. *57 rooms | C/ Jesús María 19 | tel. 9 59 12 68 99 | www.hotelconvento aracena.es | Moderate–Expensive*

FINCA VALBONO

Located just outside of Aracena, this beautifully restored estate is now a lovely three-star hotel. *30 rooms and apartments | Ctra. Carboneras, km 1 | tel. 9 59 12 77 11 | www.fincavalbono.com | Moderate*

INFORMATION

Oficina de Turismo (tel. 6 63 93 78 77) at the entrance to Gruta de las Maravillas. Natural park information: *Centro de Interpretación del Parque Natural (Plaza Alta | halfway to the castle) www.aracena.es*

WHERE TO GO

INSIDER TIP ALMONASTER LA REAL
(144 C2) (*∅ B3*)

27 km/17 mi west of Aracena is one of the most beautiful towns in the Sierra (pop. 1800). Here, you'll find a fortress and 10th-century mosque sitting enthroned on high ground. From the ⚜ minaret, you'll have a view second to none, overlooking a 19th-century bullring that hugs the fortress walls like a massive swallow's nest. For accommodation, contact the hotel and restaurant *Casa García (22 rooms | Av. San Martín 2 | tel. 9 59 14 31 09 | Budget)*. Nearby is Jabugo, the town where Spain's most famous ham is

---

⭐ **Sierra de Aracena**
Forested, rugged, mountainous area with vultures, eagles and wolves. Perfect for outdoor types → p. 32

⭐ **Mezquita in Córdoba**
This Catholic cathedral was built among a magical Moorish forest of stone columns → p. 39

⭐ **Barrio Santa Cruz**
Seville's fairy-tale-like former Jewish quarter → p. 49

⭐ **Catedral and Giralda**
Seville – a Catholic cathedral watched over by an old minaret → p. 49

⭐ **Madinat al-Zahra**
Wander around this beautiful palace-city where the caliphs of Córdoba once lived in extravagant luxury → p. 42

⭐ **Real Alcázar**
A Christian king had a Moorish jewel and delightful gardens created in the heart of Seville → p. 52

⭐ **Parque Nacional Coto de Doñana**
This national park in the Guadalquivir estuary is Europe's largest bird sanctuary → p. 47

MARCO POLO HIGHLIGHTS

made. The pigs here eat nothing but holm oak acorns for the last three months of their life.

FUENTEHERIDOS AND ALÁJAR
(144 C2) *(ØØ C3)*

Surrounded by chestnut and holm oak forests, *Fuenteheridos* is a 600-soul village 11 km/7 mi west of Aracena. Pouring water out of twelve large taps, a fountain in the middle of El Coso represents the village's abundant water supply. Although the narrow lanes are hard to drive down, the rustic *Restaurante Biarritz* offers great local Sierra cuisine, like scambled eggs with mushrooms *(C/ Charneca 13 | tel. 9 59 12 50 88 | Budget–Moderate)*. Nearby is the family-run *Hostal Carballo (7 rooms | C/ La Fuente 16 | tel. 9 59 12 51 08 | www.hostalcarballo.com | Budget)*. 5 km/3 mi out of Fuenteheridos is the town of *Alájar*. Enjoy a cup of coffee and stay cool in the church's shade. Spend the night in the town's eco-friendly country hotel and restaurant: ☺ INSIDER**TIP** *Posada de San Marcos (6 rooms | C/ Colón 12 | tel. 9 59 12 57 12 | posadasalajar.com | Moderate)*. Guests are invited to a group yoga lesson each morning.

INSIDER**TIP** LINARES DE LA SIERRA
(144 C2) *(ØØ C3)*

A well-marked hiking trail takes you from Aracena to Linares 6 km/3.7 mi away. This picturesque village still has two communal places where the locals wash their clothes (*lavaderos*) and a plaza that becomes a bullfighting arena during the Fiesta de San Juan in June.

MINAS DE RIOTINTO
(144–145 C–D3) *(ØØ C3)*

The *Río Tinto* (EN: the red river) has been used as a surface mine for 5000 years to dig iron ore. This battered landscape is still impressive, especially when observed from the ☙ lookout point north of Minas de Riotinto and 31 km/19.3 mi south of Aracena on A 461. Although the river banks are less inviting to see up close, the mining museum *Museo Minero* is worth the trip *(daily 10.30am–3pm and 4pm–7pm, mid-July–mid-Sept till 8pm | admission 5 euros | parquemineroderio tinto.es)*. They offer railway tours through the mines.

CÓRDOBA

▓▓ MAP INSIDE BACK COVER
(147 E4) *(ØØ G3)* **In the beautiful city of Córdoba, visitors from all over the world fill the narrow streets of the Judería quarter while jostling for space around the Mezquita. But just a few steps away from the 1000-year-old mosque, the tourist crowds disperse. The third-largest city in Andalucía (pop. 330,000) is also known for its peacefully secluded patios.**

It's worth coming to Córdoba just to see the Mezquita. The Arabs' legacy made Córdoba one of the most important cities at the turn of the first century. But there is a lot more to do. Sit in one of the bars next to the church at Plaza Trinidad and watch

---

🏛 WHERE TO START?
Mezquita: After visiting the city's must-see mosque-cathedral, you'll have plenty more sights to see in the city. If you come by car, park in either the car park *La Ribera (Paseo de la Ribera 1)* or in *La Mezquita (C/ Cairuan 1)*. If you arrive by train, take, e.g. bus line 3 from the main train station and get off at Glorieta de Media Luna.

Calleja de las Flores in Córdobas Judería: a paradise for garden pot lovers

how lively the locals communicate. Next, get lost in the city's many little streets. They never seem to go where you expect; you'll be pleasantly surprised at what you'll find. Much of the city has been renovated. In 2016, an architecturally impressive culture and art exhibition centre opened called the *Espacio Andaluz de Creación Contemporánea* (C4 for short).

SIGHTSEEING

ALCÁZAR DE LOS REYES CRISTIANOS
In 1236, after Ferdinand 'the Saint' put an end to 500 years of Arabian rule in Córdoba, Alfonso XI had the 'Palace of the Christian Monarchs' built. In the 14th century, it was unusual for a Christian palace to have royal baths installed. These *Baños Reales* were influenced by Moorish architecture *(admission 2.50 euros)*. The *Torre de la Inquisición* is a reminder of the palace's dark past. It used to be the seat of the Inquisition be-

tween 1482 and 1821. After touring the Alcázar, walk through the beautiful, Moor-ish-styled garden. *Mid-Sept–mid-June Tue–Fri 8.30am–8.45pm, Sat 8.30am–4.30pm, Sun 8.30am–2.30pm, mid-June–mid-Sept Tue–Sat 8.30am–3pm, Sun 8.30am–2.30pm | admission 4.50 euros*

INSIDER TIP CAPILLA DE SAN BARTOLOMÉ
Also known as *Capilla Mudéjar*, this early 15th-centruy burial chapel is richly decorated with azulejos and yeseria plasterwork. While you're here, get a closer look at the Arabic scripts inscribed in kufic. *Mid-Sept–mid-June Tue–Sat 10.30am–1.30pm and 3.30pm–6.30pm, Sun 10.30am–1.30pm, mid-June–mid-Sept Tue–Sun 10.30am–1.30pm | admission 1.50 euros, Sat/Sun for 2 euros | Plaza Maimónides*

CENTRO FLAMENCO FOSFORITO
In the 15th century, Miguel de Cervantes spent the night in Posada del Potro.

The columns of the Mezquita: 345, 346, 347... forget it! Counting all 856 of them is just too daunting

After mentioning this inn in his novel 'Don Quijote', the name became eternalised. Today, the inn houses an exciting flamenco centre. The rooms present the artists made legendary in this Andalucían art form. Come and listen to differing styles of flamenco, learn about the specific techniques applied and try clapping along to the *compás,* or beat of flamenco music. The centre also puts on concerts. *Tue–Fri 8.30am–7.30pm, Sat/ Sun 8.30am–2.30pm | free admission | Plaza del Potro | www.centroflamenco fosforito.cordoba.es*

JUDERÍA

In the mid-10th century during Caliphate rule, many Jews moved to Córdoba and resided around the Mezquita. The period of religious tolerance ended in the 14th century under Christian rule. In 1391, the worst pogrom took place. By 1492, all of the Jews had been driven out on the orders of the Catholic king. Today, the former Jewish quarter is a Unesco World Heritage Site and visited by many tourists. Experience the narrow streets, whitewashed buildings and flower-filled courtyards. Make sure to walk down *Calleja de las Flores* (flower lane). The only synagogue standing in Andalucía is at *Calle Judíos 20 (Tue–Sat 9.30am–2pm, 3.30pm–5.30pm, Sun 9.30am–5pm | free admission for EU citizens).* This Mudéjar-style building was built in 1315 during the rule of Alfonso XI.

The museum *Casa de Sefarad* is in a historical building where you'll learn how the Sephardim, the Jews of Spain forced into exile, lived in 1492 *(daily 10am– 6pm | admission 4 euro | www.casadese farad.es).* Each room explains how they lived and their rituals. Concerts also take place here.

On the south-eastern side, opposite the entrance, is the *mihrab*, the magnificent prayer niche that was added during the second extension in the mid-10th century. The last building phase, when the Mezquita was extended to the northeast, is the least inspiring. The arches over the columns here are only painted. After capturing Córdoba in 1236, the Christians used the Mezquita as a church. Over the next 300 years, they were content with simply adding small chapels that hardly effected the overall impression of the former mosque. However, in the 16th century, the bishop Alonso Manrique insisted on a cathedral being built. Despite fierce opposition from the local populace, a Renaissance church was planted in the middle of the Mezquita. To this day, nobody has dared remove the result of this act of architectural sacrilege. *March–Oct Mon–Sat 10am–7pm, Sun 8.30am–11.30am and 3pm–7pm, Nov–Feb Mon–Sat 10am–6pm, Sun 8.30am–11.30am and 3pm–6pm | admission 10 euros, entry to climb the bell tower 2 euros | www.mezquitadecordoba.org*

MEZQUITA ★ ●

Walk through the Puerta de las Palmas and into the mosque. You're now standing in a magical forest of columns standing in long rows with red-and-white double arches spanned above each other. At first, the square-shaped Mezquita appears to be perfectly symmetrical. But, with every step, the building's shape becomes more complex. After buying the basilica from the Christians, the Moorish rulers erected a mosque in 785. It wasn't until the turn of the first century and after three expansions that the Mezquita reached the dimensions it has today. If you walk anti-clockwise around the building, you'll be able to trace its construction in chronological order. The columns in the first quarter behind the entrance are Roman and Visigothic structures; the arches above them are made of yellowy-white sandstone and red brick.

MUSEO ARQUEOLÓGICO

Córdoba's fascinating archaeological museum boasts Neolithic ceramics, limestone sculptures from the Iberian period (6th–3rd centuries BC), Roman mosaics and Islamic art from Córdoba's heyday around the turn of the first millennium. *Mid-Sept–mid-June Tue–Sat 9am–8pm, Sun 9am–3pm, mid-June–mid-Sept Tue–Sun 9am–3pm | free admission for EU citizens | Plaza de Jerónimo Páez 7*

PALACIO DE VIANA

Córdoba's most magnificent palace dates back to the 14th century and has been expanded upon many times since. Today, it displays 12 courtyards and a beautiful garden. *Noches de Viana*, an arts festival for book readings, concerts and exhibitions, takes place in April and during the summer months *(admission 10 euros). July/Aug Tue–Sun 9am–3pm, Sept–June Tue–Sat 10am–7pm, Sun 10am–3pm | admission 8 euros, courtyards only 5 euros | Plaza Don Gome 2 | www.palaciodeviana. com*

PLAZA DEL POTRO

Built in the Spanish, late Gothic, Plateresque style, this inviting plaza in the middle of the city is dominated by the façade of the *Museo de Bellas Artes*. The statue of a colt with its front legs raised above the Renaissance fountain in the middle of the square is one of Córdoba's emblems.

TORRE DE LA CALAHORRA ☆

The popular *Museo Vivo de al-Andalus* is located in a former defense tower from 1369. You'll learn about the life of the Muslims, Christians and Jews during Caliphate rule. But the presentation is more romantic than informative. From here, enjoy a picture-postcard view looking over the Guadalquivir and the *Puente Romano* – a Roman bridge near the Mezquita that sits on foundations built during Emperor Augustus' rule. *May–Sept daily 10am–2pm and 4.30pm–8.30pm, Oct–April 10am–6pm | admission 4.50 euros | www.torrecalahorra.es*

FOOD & DRINK

INSIDER TIP AMALTEA

Modern Mediterranean cuisine and – a rarity in Andalucía – delicious salads. On the road along the banks of the Guadalquivir. *Closed Sun evening | Ronda de Isasa 10 | tel. 9 57 49 19 68 | Budget–Moderate*

LA BICICLETA

You'll be craving a vitamin boost after seeing the fresh fruits and vegatables on display here! This alternative juice bar also offers delicious tapas, cake and many vegan options. The staff is friendly and helpful. *Daily | C/ Cardenal González 1 | tel. 6 66 54 46 90 | Moderate*

CASA PEPE DE LA JUDERÍA

Here, you'll find traditional cuisine served in a cosy environment. The tapas and dishes are outstanding, and, if you're lucky, you may even be seated on their rooftop terrace. *Daily | C/ Romero 1 | tel. 9 57 20 07 44 | Moderate–Expensive*

EL CHURRASCO ●

Antiques give this restaurant close to the Mezquita its special atmosphere. Steaks from cattle reared in the Valle de los Pedroches are very popular. *C/ Romero 16 | tel. 9 57 29 08 19 | www.elchurrasco.com | Expensive*

SHOPPING

The *Zoco Municipal*, a market hall for hand-crafted products opposite the synagogue, looks like a tourist trap at first, but it's not! Filigree silver work, for which Córdoba is internationally renowned, can be found, e.g. in the *Joyería Maimónides (C/ Romero 5)*. The locals head for the *Cordobán Meryan* workshops *(Calleja de las Flores 2)* for pure leather articles. The *Calle Cardenal González*, below the Mezquita, with its many lovely boutiques, is an alternative to the souvenir shops in the Jewish quarter.

LEISURE

HAMMAM AL ÁNDALUS ●

This hammam in Córdoba is one of the most beautiful Arabian spas known. They offer Arab bath sessions and a number of massage treatments. *Entry every two hours 10am–10pm | admission 28 euros,* with massage 41 euros | C/ Corregidor Luis de la Cerda 51 | tel. 9 57 48 47 46 | www. hammamalandalus.com

ENTERTAINMENT

The lounge/night café *Sojo Ribera* on the roof of the multi-storey car park *La Herradura (Paseo de la Ribera 1)* at the Miraflores bridge over the Guadalquivir is smart and 'in'. Equally chic and especially cool is the gastro bar INSIDER TIP *Fusión by Sojo*, just a few yards further down the street on the corner of the Plaza del Potro. Lively pubs in the Old Town can be found on the giant rectangular *Plaza de la Corredera* with its long arcade and *Av. Gran Capitán* near San Hipólito church. Good flamenco shows are held in ⬤ *Tablao Cardenal (Feb–Nov Mon–Sat 10.30pm | admission 23 euros | C/ Buen Pastor 2 | www.tablaocardenal.es).* Another great location is the *Centro Flamenco Fosforito,* where flamenco concerts are put on at least once every week.

WHERE TO STAY ⬤

BALCÓN DE CÓRDOBA ⬤

Which hotel is the most beautiful in the city? With its quiet and relaxing atmosphere, three patios, sun terrace and discreet charm, Balcón de Córdoba is at the top of many people's list. *10 rooms | C/ Encarnación 8 | tel. 9 57 49 84 78 | www.balcondecordoba.com | Expensive*

CASA DE LOS AZULEJOS ⬤

This hotel in Córdoba aims to be more authentic than luxurious. It should have style, be rustic and have the obligatory patio, preferably with a rippling fountain. The goal is to give you the feeling the locals have while living here. Sound interesting? Then Case de los Azulejos is the place for you. *9 rooms | C/ Fernando*

Clapping is just part of the flamenco dancer's job

Colón 5 | tel. 9 57 47 00 00 | www.casade losazulejos.com | Moderate

HACIENDA POSADA DE VALLINA

Perfectly situated near the Mezquita and yet on a quiet side street. Very small, yet classically and comfortably furnished rooms. *21 rooms | C/ Corregidor Luis de la Cerda 83 | tel. 9 57 49 87 50 | www.hh posadadevallina.es | Budget–Moderate*

HOSPES PALACIO DEL BAILÍO

Córdoba's most exclusive hotel is on the northern edge of the Old Town. With its romantic interior, the palace grounds enclose four atmospheric patios. *53 rooms | C/ Ramírez de las Casas*

Deza 10–12 | tel. 9 57 49 89 93 | www. hospes.es | Expensive

OFICINAS DE TURISMO
Plaza del Triunfo | tel. 9 02 20 17 74 | www. turismodecordoba.org; Turismo de Andalucía (C/ Torrijos 10/opposite the Mezquita) | tel. 9 57 35 51 79); other information stands can be found in the station, on the Plaza de las Tendillas and at the Alcázar.

WHERE TO GO

ALMODÓVAR DEL RÍO
(147 D4) (*M F3*)
25 km/15.5 mi west of Córdoba, this beautiful little town of 8000 inhabitants is tucked away in the Guadalquivir valley and dominated by a massive, crenellated 12th-century Moorish fortress *(Mon–Fri 11am–2.30pm and 4pm–7pm, April–Sept till 8pm, Sat/Sun 11am–7pm, April–Sept till 8pm | admission 8 euros | castillode almodovar.com).* For good food at affordable prices, the restaeunt *La Taberna* is recommended. *Closed Mon, in July also Sun | C/ Antonio Machado 24 | tel. 9 57 71 36 84 | www.latabernadealmodovardel rio.com | Moderate*

MADINAT AL-ZAHRA ⭐
(147 D4) (*M G3*)
Feeling quite powerful, the Emir of Córdoba, Abd Ar Rahman III of the Umayyad dynasty self-proclaimed the title Caliph in 929. To demonstrate his power, he ordered a new seat of parliament to be built beyond the gates of Córdoba – the Madinat al-Zahra, i.e. *Medina Azahara*. This led to a fairy tale-like palace-city being erected 10 km/6.2 mi west of Córdoba. Word of its extravagant luxury soon spread worldwide. However, tension within the new Caliphate led to this newly completed splendour being destroyed by forces opposed to the Umayyad dynasty in 1010. Excavation of the site started in 1911. Two buildings have been partially rebuilt and give some idea of the magnificent structures lost – the *Salón Rico*, or the *Salón de Abd Ar Rahman III*, and the *Edifício Basilical Superior*. Visits start at the new information and research centre, where, apart from watching a film, you can marvel at selected finds in the museum. A stop at the museum shop is also worthwhile. A shuttle bus *(2.10 euros)* runs every 30 minutes from the car park to the excavation site. *April–mid-June Tue–Sat 9am–8.30pm, mid-June–mid-Sept 9am–3.30pm, mid-Sept–March 9am–6.30pm, Sun all year round 9am–8.30pm | free admission for EU citizens | www.medinaazahara.org*
Every Tuesday to Sunday, a bus runs from Córdoba to Madinat al-Zahra. It starts in Córdoba at 10.15am and 11am. The bus stops are located at *Paseo de la Victoria* near the *Glorieta Hospital Cruz Roja* and at *Paseo de la Victoria* across from the *Mercado Victoria*. Tickets are available to purchase *(9 euros)* at the tourist information point or can be found online at *www. reservasturismodecordoba.org.*

INSIDER TIP SIERRA SUBBÉTICA
(147 F5–6) (*M H4*)
In the village of *Zuheros*, men gather on the ☀ Plaza de la Paz below a 9th-century castle overlooking vast fields (*campiñas*) of olive groves. This whitewashed village clings to the hillside of the Sierra Subbética – a fascinating, barren, mountainous area some distance from the main road. Linking Córdoba and Granada, most tourists pass by this area but, if in a hurry, miss out on seeing dream-like villages like *Zuheros* and *Luque* and the elaborate Baroque buildings along the *Ruta del Barroco*.

100 km/64.6 mi southeast of Córdoba and with 23,500 inhabitants, *Priego de Córdoba* is the main town in the Sierra Subbética. Its Old Town is whitewashed and perched romantically on the side of a rocky plateau. The cosy restaurant *El Aljibe* sits in the shade of the Arabian fortress *(closed Mon | C/ Abad Palomino 16 | tel. 9 57 70 18 56 | Budget–Moderate)*. Not far from there, among the tangle of narrow alleyways in the Old Town, is one of the nicest guesthouses in the area –

along a former railway line. For more information, go to *Oficina de Turismo (Plaza de la Constitución 3 | tel. 9 57 70 06 25 | www.turismodepriego.com)*

HUELVA

(144 B4) *(𝄐 B5)* **This provincial capital with 145,000 inhabitants is the economic centre of Costa de la Luz, the western region of Andalucía.**

A living-room view in Zuheros: standing strong on a hill of the Sierra Subbética

La Posada Real (7 rooms | C/ Real 14 | tel. 9 57 54 19 10 | www.laposadareal. com | Budget). You can get first-class organic olive oil at ⊙ *Vizcántar (Ctra. Zagrilla)* and in Baena at *Núñez del Prado (Av. de Cervantes 15)*. The oil mills are open to the public. On the northern edge of the Sierra, there is a cycle route called the *Vía Verde de la Subbética*, which runs

During Franco's rule, this city was developed as the centre of the petrochemical industry. Two other economically important industries are the fishing and strawberry industries in the local area. Unfortunately, many of the city sites were destroyed in the same earthquake that flattened Lisbon in 1755. Nevertheless, the city still remains a pleasant, lively and comfortable place to visit. If you prefer standing clear of the tourists, this city and its surroundings will please you. The west has a much different character than the eastern regions of

LA FONDA DE MARÍA MANDAO
This restaurant's green, tiled façade and red, wooden doors, make you feel wel-

A pilgrimage to Virgen in El Rocío: the Wild West, hair gel and bellowing skirts

Andalucía. The untouched dunes and the marshland (*marisma*) in the Coto de Doñana National Park are one of a kind. History was made in Palos de la Frontera when Columbus left this former fishing village to begin his first voyage of discovery. In Punta Umbria, you'll find a seaside resort with sandy beaches that stretch out along the coastline.

comed before you even step inside. The menu's delicious starters and *raciones* can be enjoyed inside or outside. The burger made with *ibérico* ham and mushrooms is especially tasty. *Closed Sun | C/ Vázquez López 11 | tel. 9 59 25 78 93 | Budget–Moderate*

SIGHTSEEING

BARRIO REINA VICTORIA
Located north of the centre between the avenues Alcalde Federico Molina and Guatemala, this architecturally interesting British workers' settlement was built in 1917 by the Riotinto mining company.

WHERE TO STAY

TARTESSOS
Although this 4-star hotel is located in the centre, it remains calm and relaxing. They offer their guests wonderful business facilities, a gym, bikes for rent and even a putting green. *100 rooms | Av. Martín Alonso Pinzón 13 | tel. 9 02 93 24 24 | www.eurostarstartessos.com | Moderate*

INFORMATION

OFICINA DE TURISMO
C/ Jesús Nazareno 21 | tel. 9 59 65 02 00 |
www.turismohuelva.org

WHERE TO GO

AYAMONTE (144 A4) (*m A5*)
The galleries of the old warehouses on the banks of the Río Guadiana are a reminder of the times when goods were ferried to and from Portugal by ship. Nowadays, almost everything goes by motorway across the suspension bridge over the river. 50 km/31 mi west of Huelva, with 21,000 inhabitants, the town's glorious centre resembles the neighbouring country of Portugal with its narrow, traffic-free lanes. The people living in the Vila Real Santo António enjoy coming to the centre to shop. Serving delicious fish and rice dishes, the *Casa Barberi (daily | Paseo de la Ribera 12 | tel. 9 59 47 02 89 | Moderate)* has been open since 1917. To go swimming, both locals and visitors drive 7 km/4.3 mi to the *Urbanización Isla Canela*. The hotels and blocks of flats here were designed in a way to avoid the monotony typically seen in planned communities. The main attraction is without doubt the vast beach and the sandbank that stretches out into the sea. Information: *Oficina de Turismo (C/ Huelva 27 | tel. 9 59 32 07 37)*

EL ROCÍO (145 D5) (*m C5*)
With 1500 inhabitants, this famous place of pilgrimage lies 65 km/40 mi east of Huelva. The charming landscape is like the Wild West with its sandy paths and wooden verandas. The golden garments of the Virgen del Rocío are in stark contrast to the plain, white-painted church. The first chapel was built here at the end of the 13th century to honour the 'Virgin of the Dew'. This place of worship, however, dates back to 1961. Each year during Pentecost, some 100 holy brotherhoods *(hermandades)* and one million others make the pilgrimage to El Rocío at Whitsun. Just beyond the village, flamingos can be seen wading through the *marismas*. For good regional cooking at moderate prices, the hotel restaurant *Toruño* is recommended *(closed Tue | 30 rooms | Plaza del Acebuchal 22 | tel. 9 59 44 24 22 | www.toruno.es | Moderate)*

MATALASCAÑAS AND MAZAGÓN (144 C5) (*m B5*)
The holiday resort *Matalascañas* was built at the end of the 1960s on the southwestern coastline of Doñana National Park on the Costa de la Luz. Sevillians come here to swim in summer, so do expect a large crowd unless you are visiting in winter. Here you can take a walk along the dunes and cross wooden foot bridges. Those wanting to avoid

LOW BUDGET

Looking for bargains? Then head down to the Thursday flea market in the Calle Feria in Seville's Old Town.

For really cheap appetisers and beer, you'll want to go to the popular tapa's chain *100 Montaditos (www.100montaditos.com)*. They can be found in all the big cities.

Serving up a marvellous midday meal for only 14 euros, *La Taberna del Alabardero (C/ Zaragoza 20 | tel. 9 54 50 27 21)* is a delicious restaurant open from Mon–Fri in Seville.

tourists should go west to INSIDER TIP *Playa de Mazagón*, a less-crowded, sandy beach. It's 23 km/14.3 mi long, up to 120 m/394 ft wide and located at the foot of a sandy cliff that was once a shifting sand dune. The cliff is more than 100 m/328 ft high. From the *Cuesta Maneli* car park *(off the A 494 at km 39)*, you can walk to the beach via the 1.2 km/0.75 mi long boardwalk crossing the dunes. The beach is also reachable via the approach road to the Parador in Mazagón (20 km/12.5 mi southeast of Huelva). Just outside Mazagón is the lovely *Parador (63 rooms | Ctra. A 494, at km 30 | tel. 9 59 53 63 00 | www.parador. es | Expensive)*, which was built at the end of the 1960s in the middle of a pine forest on a hillside overlooking the sea.

PALOS DE LA FRONTERA AND THE COLUMBUS ROUTE (144 B4) *(ΜΟ B5)*
Christopher Columbus (or Cristóbal Colón in Spanish) set out on his first voyage of discovery on 3 August 1492. He started 13 km/8 mi southeast of Huelva in a village of whitewashed houses at the mouth of the Río Tinto. This journey was to take him westwards in search of a passage to India. The last church service before sailing was held at the *Iglesia San Jorge*. The ship lay at anchor a little down river. Having silted up, the harbour no longer exists. After fleeing Portugal in 1485, the first place the native of Genoa sought out was the *Monasterio de La Rábida (Tue–Sat 10am–1pm and 4pm– 6.15pm, April–Oct till 7pm, Sun 10.45am– 1pm | admission 3.50 euros)*. Here is where he later planned his first voyage. A 14th-century alabaster statue of the Virgin Mary is noteworthy. Columbus discussed his plans with the padres in the chapter house. The *Jardín Botánico José Celestino Mutis* is at the foot of the hill and boasts plants from the Iberian Peninsula and Latin America. The main attractions are the replicas of Columbus' three ships in the *Muelle de las Carabelas (mid-June–mid-Sept Tue–Sun 10am– 9.30pm, mid-Sept–mid-June 9.30am– 7.30pm | admission 3.55 euros)*. A medieval village and several Indians' huts set the period scene, while the main building contains maps and information boards about Columbus' three voyages.

FOR BOOKWORMS & FILM BUFFS

The Hand of Fatima – This almost 1000-page tome by the internationally acclaimed author Ildefonso Falcones takes the reader back to the Kingdom of Granada in 16th-century Andalucía.

The Ignorance of Blood – Robert Wilson's 2009 psychological thriller takes place in Seville with Inspector Jefe Javier Falcón. Investigating a terrorist attack, a dead gangster and a suitcase full of cash leads to the Russian mafia.

Flamenco, Flamenco – This 2010 film by Carlos Sauras brings the best musicians and dancers to the big screen (e.g. Paco de Lucía, Sara Baras, Eva Yerbabuena).

Knight and Day – This American action comedy from 2010 was partly filmed in Andalucía and stars Tom Cruise and Cameron Diaz. You'll be entertained as they roam through the same Old Towns of Cádiz and Seville that you've already been to yourself.

Take a tour through the Doñana National Park in an off-road bus

Located on the Columbus Route, the neighbouring, whitewashed village of *Moguer* offers beautiful accommodation. Surrounded by three patios, the country hotel *Plaza Escribano* is both affordable and comfortable *(20 rooms | C/ Lora Tamayo 5 | tel. 9 59 37 30 63 | www.hotel plazaescribano.com | Budget)*.

PARQUE NACIONAL COTO DE DOÑANA ★ (145 D5–6) (*m* C5–6)

One of the most important areas of natural beauty in Europe lies east of Huelva in the Guadalquivir delta – Permanently flooded swathes of land *(marismas)* behind huge migrating dunes, provide an ideal environment for more than 300 types of birds, ranging from the purple heron to the pied avocet. With over 209 sq mi of nature, one can really escape the outside world. Even the imperial eagle and Iberian lynx have found refuge here.

For centuries, the Doñana was an exclusive hunting ground *(coto)* until biologists drew attention to its unprecedented ecological importance in the 1950s. It became a national park in 1969 and was declared a UNESCO World Heritage Site in 1994.

The peace and quiet of the Doñana is interrupted twice a day by off-road busses taking visitors around the southern part of the park. This 4-hour excursion is well worth the ride *(May–mid-Sept Mon–Sat 8.30am and 5pm, mid-Sept– April Tue–Sun 8.30am and 3pm | fare 30 euros | departing from the Acebuche visitor centre on the western edge of the park | tel. 9 59 43 04 32)*. The half-day and full-day tours *(from 180 euros)* for four to six people are also worthwhile. The information centre and restaurant *El Acebuche (www.donanavisitas.es | www. donana.es)* is open daily from 8am to 7pm. Other visitor centres on the A 483 are *La Rocina* and *Centro de Visitantes Palacio del Acebrón*. Both visiting centres are open daily from 9am to 3pm and 4pm to 7pm and located near a number of hiking trails leading into the peripheral areas of the national park.

Seville: 21st-century Las Setas (front) vs the 12-century Giralda (background/left)

SEVILLE

◼◼◼ **MAP INSIDE BACK COVER**
◼◼◼ (145 E4) *(ᗰ D4)* **Youths on mopeds in jeans and t-shirts wind their way between the traffic on the Avenida de la Constitución.**

The sounds typical of this city include the rattle of two-stroke engines, trotting horses, flamenco music blaring out of the bars and the long drawn-out call of blind lottery-ticket sellers. With a population of 700,000, this city is the fourth largest in Spain and bursting with life. However, the Sevillians are never hectic. The sun, shining a merciless white at midday and bathing the streets in a reddish hue in the evenings, curbs any restlessness. A labyrinth of narrow streets, squares, monuments, lush gardens and blocks of flats crowned by roof terraces can be found around the Giralda. This major landmarks was originally a minaret and later converted into a bell tower for the cathedral. Seville shined brightest at the turn of the first century during Moorish rule and a good 500 years later after the discovery and the exploitation of Latin America.

But the city is not only known for its great past. The world looked to Seville during the 1992 Expo when a new district was created on the peninsula La Cartuja. In 2016, the city's first skyscraper was built. The office tower is 180 m/590.5 ft high. More exciting for visitors and directly next to the skyscraper is the brand new CaixaForum. Seville is marked by how it blends the old with the new. No matter the age, the people of Seville view their traditions as holy, including the feria festival and the precessions during *Semana Santa*. Just as in their craftmanship, these traditions spark new ideas, projects, fashion design and art, and this innovation comes not only from the many students roaming the city. If you're look-

María Luisa. The park is also ideal for relaxing, reading and reflecting upon whether there's perhaps another city in the world comparable to Seville. For 13.33 euros, you can ride a bike for 7 days (150 euros for the deposit). Or you can pay by the hour: the first 30 minutes are free; the first hour costs 1 euro and any additional hour costs 2.04 euros. Practical descriptions of the tours offered are available at the tourist information point.

ing for cool bars and interesting shops, the neighbourhoods of *La Macarena* and *Triana* are your best bet.

Locals and visitors use the bike rental system to get around the city. Sevici *(www.sevici.es)* has 250 bike rental stations in the city, including around the new financial and liesure areas along the Guadalquivir River and in the lovely Parque

SIGHTSEEING

BARRIO SANTA CRUZ ★
Wander around this fairy-tale suburb in the shadow of the Reales Alcázares. Head off without a map and explore the narrow streets. Gander at the whitewashed houses, stop for a cup of coffee in one of the bars or visit the little shops. In the *Calle Lope de Rueda*, potted plants turn the road into a cosy courtyard perfect for locals to meet for a chat. The Jewish quarter was the scene of a pogrom in 1391 and the expulsion of its residents in 1492.

CASA DE PILATOS
What a beautiful palace! An enchanted place that opens its doors to a distant past filled with dreamy courtyards, stunning Mudéjar decor and an impressive collection of paintings and antique furniture. This 16th-century Renaissance palace is like a fantasy land. No wonder so many films (e.g. 'Lawrence of Arabia') have used it as their backdrop. *Daily 9am–6pm, April–Oct till 7pm | admission 8 euros | Plaza de Pilatos | www.fundacionmedinaceli.org*

CATEDRAL AND GIRALDA ★
'Let us build a church so beautiful and so great that those who see it will think we were mad.' This target set by a member

---

CITY WHERE TO START?
To the **cathedral**! Near here is where you'll find the Reales Alcázares and barrio Santa Cruz with its many tapas bars. The Guadalquivir and Torre del Oro are also not far from here. Drivers should leave their cars in one of the car parks – the Paseo Colón car park is easy to find on the riverside road. Bus route C5 and tramline 1 stop close to the cathedral.

From the minarett to the bell tower: the Giralda represents Andalucía's religious diversity

of the cathedral chapter was taken up by the builders in the 15th century. Together, they erected the largest Gothic ecclesiastical building in the world: the *Catedral de Sevilla*. Since 1902, just inside the south door, Christopher Columbus' mortal remains, although the skeleton is not complete, have been housed in a sarcophagus supported by four bearers sculpted in stone. In 2006, DNA tests confirmed this. The main attraction is the high altar in the interior of the building with its dizzying wealth of ornamentation that took 100 years to complete. Typical to Andalucía, the cathedral was built on a mosque site with an orange tree courtyard and the ☀ *Giralda*, a minaret from the 12th century. When it was turned into a bell tower in the 16th century, the minaret was given a Renaissance-style spire, crowned with a 4 m/13 ft high figure holding a standard and palm twig. Since the tower (97 m/318 ft in height) turns in the wind, it was named *Giraldillo* (*girar:* 'to turn'). A sloping ramp brings you to the tip of the Giralda, where you'll

have the best view of Seville. *Mon 11am–3.30pm, Tue–Sat 11am–5pm, Sun 2.30pm–6pm | admission 9 euros | www.catedral desevilla.es*

ISLA LA CARTUJA

The 1992 Expo took place in the northwest of Seville. Today, the Expo lake is a leisure park called *Isla Mágica*. Designed by architect Santiago Calatrava and in the shape of a massive harp, the distinctive bridge of *Puente del Alamillo* spans north of the park over the Guadalquivir. To the south is the former charterhouse monastery *Monasterio de Santa María de las Cuevas*, which houses the highly-recommended contemporary art centre *Centro Andaluz de Arte Contemporáneo (Tue–Sat 11am–9pm, Sun 10am–3.30pm | admission 3 euros, on Tue/Wed from 7pm and Sat free admission | www.caac. es)*. South of the *Puente de la Cartuja* footbridge is the 50 m/164 ft tower of the maritime museum *Pabellón de la Navegación (Nov–March Tue–Sat 10am–7.30pm, Sun 10am–3pm, April–June and*

Sept/Oct Tue–Sat 11am–8.30pm, Sun 11am–3pm, July/Aug Tue–Sun 10am–3.30pm | admission 4.90 euros | Camino de los Descubrimientos 2 | www.pabellon delanavegacion.es). Tickets for the maritime museum include access to the ❄ viewing platform. Hidden underground is the city's newest cultural landmark: the *Caixaforum Sevilla (daily 10am–8pm| admission 3 euros | Camino de los Descubrimientos | obrasocialla caixa.org).* In this cultural centre, you'll find varying art exhibitions, concerts and other cultural events.

MUELLE DE LAS DELICIAS

When the massive cruise ships are docked, it's easy to tell where the pier is. Look just south of the centre, roughly across from María Luisa Park. Here you'll also find a marine aquarium, a big wheel and plenty of outdoor dining. Many have made this their favourite summer location in Seville.

MUSEO DEL BAILE FLAMENCO

Flamenco is a combination of energy and emotion, but how do you show it in a museum? It's not that difficult when the museum's walls have a history and Cristina Hoyos, a flamenco artist who starred with Carlos Saura in the 1983 drama 'Carmen', plays a part in the exhibition. To help present the material, the exhibit uses multimedia to give you the feeling of sitting in the front row at the *tablaos*. Flamenco lessons are also available here. *Museum daily 10am–7pm, flamenco shows daily from 7pm | C/ Manuel Rojas Marcos 3 | museum admission 10 euros, combi-ticket with show 24 euros | www. museoflamenco.com*

MUSEO DE BELLAS ARTES ●

The magnificent museum of fine art is located in a 17th-century monastery and displays Spanish paintings from the 17th and 18th centuries. Painted in the Seville Art School, the priceless works presented in this museum are by, e.g. Francisco de Zurbarán, Bartolomé Esteban Murillo and Juan de Valdés Leal. *Mid-Sept–mid-June Tue–Sat 9am–8pm, Sun 9am–3pm, mid-June–mid-Sept Tue–Sun 9am–3pm | free admission for EU citizens | Plaza del Museo 9 | www.museosdeandalucia.es*

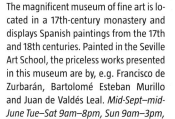
The Flamenco Museum: Embrace the spirit of this art through multimedia

PARQUE DE MARÍA LUISA ●

To reach this park, leave the Old Town and head south for a short distance. The park that was laid out for the Ibero-American Exposition in 1929. The *Plaza de España* lies rather artificially like a film set right in the middle of the park, with an imposing, semi-circular building with a diameter of 200 m/656 ft at one end. The outer walls are covered with decorative tiles depicting scenes from the history of the Spanish provinces. The benches below are perfect for lazying around.

merous symbols of Catholic Spain – the castle and the lion – as well as the motto of the Nasrid kings in Arabic script: 'There is no victor but Allah'. With its richly decorated vaulted ceiling, the *Sala de Embajadores,* the hall of the ambassadors, is one of the highlights inside. Alone, a visit to the gardens is well worth-while. They are a scented oasis of tranquillity with fountains and tiled benches plumb in the middle of the city. The atmospheric INSIDER TIP 'Alcázar Nights', with concerts after 10.30pm (doors open at 9pm) and a bar, run from

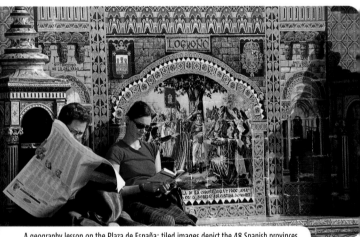

A geography lesson on the Plaza de España: tiled images depict the 48 Spanish provinces

REAL ALCÁZAR ★ ●

This royal palace complex can be a bit confusing to visitors at first. It wasn't the Arabs who had these buildings constructed in the 14th century, but the Christian King Peter the Cruel. He created a royal nest for himself and his lover. However, the builders were Moors, sent by rulers of the Nasrid dynasty from Granada. The result is the most beautiful building in the Mudéjar style anywhere. Among playful Arabian ornamentation, there are nu-

July until mid-September. Tickets costing 6 euros have to be bought during the day at the Alcázar. *Daily 9.30am–5pm, April–Sept until 7pm | admission 9.50 euros | www.alcazarsevilla.org*

SETAS DE SEVILLE

If you're looking for some shade, a market place or a panoramic terrace, the giant wooden construction on the Plaza de la Encarnación is perfect for all three. Known as *Las Setas (The Mushrooms),* this structure was designed by the German architect Jürgen Mayer H. The elevator in the basement brings you up to the restaurant or ☀ the observation deck 20 m/65 ft above ground. From here, you can walk along the footpath to see the Old Town from all angles. During construction, remnants of wall were found dating back to the Roman era. Today, in the underground aquarium, you can walk through the ruins of Seville and get an idea of how the city looked between AD 30 and AD 400. *Sun–Thu 10am–11pm, Fri/Sat 10am–11.30pm | admission 3 euros incl. complimentary drink | Plaza da la Encarnación 35 | setasdesevilla.com*

REAL MAESTRANZA BULLRING

Seville's 18th-century *plaza de toros*, seating 14,000, is the largest in Andalucía and the most important in Spain outside Madrid. *Daily 9.30am–7pm, April–Oct till 9pm, on days bullfights are held 9.30am–3pm | admission 8 euros | Paseo de Colón 12 | www.realmaestranza.com*

TORRE DEL ORO

The golden tower on the banks of the Guadalquivir was built as a defensive tower around 1220 under the Moors. Seville's second most famous landmark after the Giralda was originally covered with gilded ceramic tiles. The tower now houses the maritime museum. *Mon–Fri 9.30am–6.45pm, Sat/Sun 10.30am–6.45pm | admission 3 euros*

TRIANA

The residents from the district west of the Guadalquivir are living in their own world. Seville, from their point of view, is nothing more than some prominent section of the city. In Triana, you'll find the city's oldest church: the *Iglesia de Santa Ana* from 1280. Triana also has

exceptional nightlife and interesting shops, e.g. near the Plaza del Altozano, that sell hadicrafts and ceramics. Triana was once a hub for producing ceramics and azulejos. The Santa Ana, a former factory, was turned into the handicraft museum *Centro Cerámica Triana (Tue–Sat 11am–5.30pm, Sun 10am–2.30pm | admission 2.10 euros | C/ Antillano Campos 14)*. Here you'll find antique kilns and eye-catching ceramics that depict the history of Azulejo art. You're also welcome to have a seat in the bar INSIDER TIP *La Grande (closed Sun | C/ San Jacinto 39)*. The bar has become an institution in Triana. The locals often come here to peel a bit of shrimp and knock down a cold *caña* ('a small beer').

FOOD & DRINK

It's really a bit of a shame to spend the evening in just one restaurant. So, do as the Sevillians do and go on a tapas tour. A good place to start is the area around the Museo de Bellas Artes, Alfalfa and San Salvador squares and the barrio Santa Cruz, in particular. One bar next to another can be found in the *Calle Mateos Gago*. The *Cervecería Giralda (closed Sun | C/ Mateos Gago 1)* is a classic. The bar *Las Teresas (daily | Santa Teresa 2)* has been around for 150 years – quite unaffected by the streams of tourism. Despite the hype around this bar, *Bar Estrella (C/ Estrella 3)* has maintained its charming and rustic character. The tapas bar *El Rinconcillo (C/ Gerona y Alhóndiga 40)* has also avoided modern trends and holds true to its authentic charm. It's also claimed to be the oldest tapas bar in Andalucía, serving guests wine since 1670. Satisfying gormet tapas can be enjoyed at *Vinería San Telmo (Paseo Catalina de Ribera 4)* and *Eslava (C/ Eslava 3)*. The well-run, old-fashioned bar *Hijos Morales (C/ García de Vinuesa 11)* between the cathedral and the bullring is also well worth a visit. If you fancy a snack or a break when shopping, the charming café and bakery *La Campana (C/ Sierpes 1)* is always inviting and offers plenty of little desserts. In the gourmet market *Lonja del Barranco (C/ Arjona 28)*, you can sample the many delicacies of the south at 20 different stands.

INSIDER TIP ALBARAMA
Who knew you could eat so well in the city centre? You have to try the mini tuna burgers on bread and their tapas creations with foie gras and sweet Sherry apple slices. *Closed Sun evenings | Plaza San Francisco 5 | tel. 9 54 22 97 84 | www. restaurantealbarama.com | Moderate*

AZ-ZAIT
Don't let the rather cheesy décor fool you! The Andalucían cusine here is outstanding and affordable. *Closed Sun | Plaza San Lorenzo 1 | tel. 9 54 90 64 75 | Moderate–Expensive*

CONTENEDOR ✪
This small, informal restaurant in the Macarena district has taken slow food to another level. Enjoy local market food while observing local art on the wall. *Daily | C/ San Luis 50 | tel. 9 54 91 63 33 | restaurantecontenedor. com | Moderate*

TABERNA DEL ALABARDERO
Turn off the outside world and enjoy a meal in the city's marvellous palace. Located near the bullring, the restaurant is exquisitely old-fashioded. Each table is eloquently set, and their high cuisine is seasonally served. Wanting a romantic dinner? A table on the roof terrace should do the trick. Affordable and delicious midday meals are also available for 14 euros. *Daily | C/ Zaragoza 20 | tel. 9 54 50 27 21 | Expensive*

SHOPPING

Seville's main shopping area is around the *C/ Sierpes* and *C/ Tetuán* to the north of the town hall. Victorio & Lucchino, the internationally known fashion designers from Seville, are at *C/ Sierpes 87*. At *C/ Sierpes 70* and *75*, a large selection of *abanicos*, traditional Spanish hand fans, are for sale. Crafted items can be found in Triana on and around the streets of *Alfarería, Antillano* and *San Jorge*. Located in a former train station in Neo-Mudéjar style, the *Plaza de Armas* is a large shopping centre on the *Plaza de la Legión* that has fashion stores, cinemas and fast food places.

In La Macarena, however, the shops and boutiques on the streets on and around Feria and Regina are even more alluring. Every second Saturday, an organic market selling local goods takes place on the garden square *Alameda de Hércules*. It's called the ✪ *Feria Ecológica de Productores Locales*. You'll also find a lovely flea market every Thursday afternoon on the *Calle Feria*.

FLAMENCO COURSES

Many of the dance schools in Seville offer lessons to tourists. Some of these include the ● *Fundación Cristina Heeren (C/ Pureza 76 | www.flamencoheeren. com)*, the flamenco workshop ● *Taller Flamenco (C/ Peral 49 | www.taller flamenco.com)* and the *Museo del Baile Flamenco (see p. 51)*.

ENTERTAINMENT

Seville is famous for its nightlife. People of all ages usually spend their evenings

The barrio of Santa Cruz: life blooms in the bars and bodegas late into the night

in the bars on the *Calle Mateos Gago* next to the Giralda or in Triana around the *Puente Isabel II* and on the *Calle Betis*. In the evenings, young people meet in the city centre between the squares of Alfalfa and Salvador. Student life and the alternative scene can be found in the bars on the *Alameda de Hércules*. On some nighs, the square becomes as full as the bleacher section during an FC Sevilla home game. Popular hangout spots in summer include the terraces on the Plaza América in the Parque María Luisa and along the banks of the Guadalquivir below the Alameda de Hércules.

Start your night near the Plaza de Armas shopping centre at the small club called INSIDER TIP *Obbio (closed Sun–Thu | C/ Trastamara 29 | obbioclub.com)*. Then go to the Isla de la Cartuja to dance in the outdoor club *Antique (Tue–Sat midnight–7am | C/ Matemáticos Rey Pastor y Castro | www.antiquetheatro.com)*.

Many *tablaos* offer flamenco shows. *Los Gallos (daily 8.30pm and 10.30pm | admission 35 euros | Plaza Santa Cruz 11 | tel. 9 54 21 69 81 | www.tablaolosgallos.com)* and *El Arenal (daily 7.30pm and 9.30pm | admission 38 euros incl. a drink | C/ Rodo 7 | tel. 9 54 21 64 92 | www.tablaoelarenal.com)* are exceptional. Some flamenco shows take place in the bars *Casa Anselma* in Triana *(Mon–Sat 11.30pm–3am | C/ Pagés del Corro 49)* and the famous (but often packed) *La Carbonería (daily 8pm–3.30am | C/ Levíes 18 | tel. 9 54 21 44 60)*, north of the barrio Santa Cruz.

WHERE TO STAY

INSIDER TIP **AMADEUS**

This small hotel in the Jewish quarter and music-themed boutique is perfect for classically-trained musicians. The soundproof rooms may be used for practice or a performance. A jacuzzi is located on the roof. *14 rooms | Farnesio 6 | tel. 9 54 50 14 43 | www.hotelamadeussevilla.com* | Moderate

CASA 1800

This boutique hotel in the Santa Cruz barrio is still fairly new. You'll be impressed by the hotel's comfort and romantic interior. The beautiful roof terrace offers a view over Giralda. *24 rooms | C/ Rodrigo Caro 6 | tel. 9 54 56 18 00 | www.hotelcasa1800sevilla.com* | Expensive

CASA SACRISTÍA SANTA ANA

Located on the lively Alameda de Hércules in an old vestry, this romantic boutique hotel centres around a beautiful patio and has an extravagant neo-Baroque interior. *25 rooms | Alameda de Hércules 22 | tel. 9 54 91 57 22 | www.hotelsacristia.com* | Budget–Moderate

LAS CASAS DE LA JUDERÍA

Situated right next to the Santa María La Blanca church, this hotel originally had 27 flats. Romantic patios link the various sections of the building. A pool is located on the roof. *118 rooms | C/ Santa María la Blanca 5 | tel. 9 54 41 51 50 | www.casasypalacios.com* | Moderate–Expensive

EME CATEDRAL ●

This luxury boutique hotel is opposite the cathedral and has over 14 old town houses. The sign is hip and elegant. Four restaurants, a small spa area and a spectacular roof terrace. *63 rooms | C/ Alemanes 5 | tel. 9 54 56 00 00 | www.emecatedralhotel.com* | Expensive

OASIS

If you'd rather go out than pay for an expensive hotel, this backpacker hostel is ideal. The rooms are clean with well-made beds. A nice mini pool is on the roof terrace. Pub crawls and sightseeing tours are also offered. *9 rooms | C/ Almirante Ulloa 1 | tel. 9 55 26 26 96 | www.oasisseville.com* | Budget

INFORMATION

OFICINA DE TURISMO

Plaza del Triunfo 1 | tel. 9 54 78 75 78 | www.visitasevilla.es and *Paseo de las Delicias 9 | tel. 9 54 23 44 65*. Branches in the station and at the airport.

WHERE TO GO

CARMONA (146 B6) *(E4)*

Located about 40 km/25 mi east of Sevilla, with 29,000 inhabitants, this town is full of history. Just stroll through the historical centre; you'll find traces of Carthaginian, Roman, Moorish and medieval Christian influences. Near the Puerta de Seville are the ruins of a 9th-century Moorish fortress called *Torre del Oro (Mon–Sat 10am–6pm, Sun 10am–3pm | admission 2 euros, Mon free admission)*. Here you can enjoy a panoramic view of the city. Of all the palaces and churches, two are particularly noteworthy: the *Iglesia de San Pedro* near the Puerta de Sevilla with its Giralda-like bell tower and the *Iglesia de Santa María (Plaza del Marqués de las Torres)* with its Moorish patio. Just outside the city is Spain's most important Roman cemetery – the *Necrópolis Romana (April–mid-June Tue–Sat 9am–8pm, mid-June–mid-Sept 9am–3pm, mid-Sept–March 9am–6pm, every Sun 9am–3pm | free admission for EU citizens | Av. Jorge Bónsor 9)*. Some tombs are like subterranean palaces.
Located in a former oil mill, the *Mesón La Almazara de Carmona (daily | C/ Santa Ana 33 | tel. 9 54 19 00 76 |* Moderate*)* serves great regional cuisine. One of the most beautiful hotels in Spain is in the

14th-century Alcázar del Rey Don Pedro: ● *Parador de Carmona (63 rooms | tel. 9 54 14 10 10 | www.parador.es | Expensive)*. Just go for a cup of coffee to see it. Information: *Oficina de Turismo (Alcázar de la Puerta de Sevilla (tel. 9 54 19 09 55 | www.turismo.carmona.org)*

ITÁLICA ● (145 E4) *(Ⓜ D4)*

Take a remarkable walk through the ruins of Itálica. Founded in 206BC and located 10 km/6.2 mi northwest of Seville, just outside of *Santiponce,* this is Andalucía's most important Roman settlement. In the 1st century, later emperors like Trajan and Hadrian grew up here. Itálica's demise followed the conquest of the Iberian Peninsula by the Arabs. Excavations began in the 18th century. Attractions include the *amphitheatre* with its 25,000 seats and the *Casa del Planetario* with its well-preserved mosaic floors. *April–mid-June Tue–Sat 9am–7.30pm, mid-June–Sept Tue–Sat 9am–3.30pm, mid-Sept–March 9am–* 5.30pm, every Sun 9am–3.30pm | free admission for EU citizens

OSUNA (151 E1) *(Ⓜ F5)*

The massive Renaissance church 🞧 *La Colegiata (Tue–Sun 10am–1.30pm and 4pm–6.30pm | admission 3 euros)* towers above this little town of 18,000 inhabitants, 90 km/56 mi east of Seville. Its fortress-like façade conceals a light-filled interior with paintings by, e.g. Jusepe de Ribera. From 1549 to 1820, Osana was a university town, and it is still rich with history.

Casa Curro (closed Mon | Plaza Salitre 5 | tel. 9 55 82 07 58 | Budget) serves amazing tapas and is well known for its regional cuisine. Located in a Baroque palace, the elegant hotel *Palacio Marqués de la Gomera (20 rooms | C/ San Pedro 20 | tel. 9 54 81 22 23 | www.hotelpalaciodel marques.es | Budget–Moderate)* is worth a detour. Information: *Oficina de Turismo (C/ Sevilla 37 | tel. 9 54 81 57 32 | www. turismosuna.es)*

A mosaic in the Casa del Planetario in Itálica: this is how tilers do puzzles!

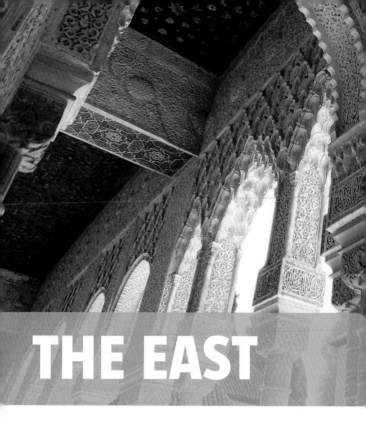

THE EAST

You'd almost think the east of Andalucía had been forgotten by the rest of the region; the capital of Seville is miles away, and the eastern provinces of Jaén, Granada and Almería are difficult to reach via public transport. Nonetheless, visitors manage to make their way here to see the Alhambra, the most exquisite architectural treasure from the Moorish period. But the excitement doesn't stop here!

There's a lot to discover in the east of Andalucía. To list a few examples, you can visit the source of the Guadalquivir in the Jaén province. It's located in the Sierra de Cazorla, where the river then twists and turns towards Córdoba. Along its banks are a slew of olive trees that grow up into the mountains of Jaén, the olive oil capital of the world. Further in the southeast, however, the soil becomes too barren to plant these fairly undemanding trees; there's only desert in the eastern part of the Granada and Almería provinces. Although the Almería coast is fascinating to see, parts of this area depress environmentalists. Nicknamed the *Costa del Plástico* by the locals, the Almería coast is covered with miles of plastic sheets for intensive farming. North African and Eastern European migrant workers plant and harvest produce here. The highest mountain on the Iberian Peninsula is east of Granada and located right in the middle of the Sierra Nevada. 3481 m/11,420 ft high, the *Mulhacén* boasts a skiing area just 40 km/25 mi from the beaches of the Costa Tropical.

Moorish architectural wonders –
the Alhambra is just one of the fascinating
buildings surrounded by incredible scenery

ALMERÍA

(155 D5) *(⟨ N6⟩)* **Although the provincial capital of Almería (pop. 195,000) is incomparable to other cities like Seville, Granada or Córdoba, it's still very much worth the trip.**

The main attraction in this port city is the Alcazaba fortress. The Old Town is dominated by a huge 16th-century cathedral, and the port boasts the monstrous steel structure *El Cable Inglés.* Constructed in

WHERE TO START?
Plaza de Estación: Anyone arriving by train or bus should go from the station square to the Gregorio Marañón bus stop. From here, take the no. 11 bus to the historical city centre. Drivers should head for one of the multi-storey car parks nearby – there are two on the Avenida García Lorca. The Old Town is not far from here.

View from the Moorish fortress of Alcazaba: Almería sits below

1904, it used to load cargo onto ships. Today, it represents the industrial culture.

ALCAZABA

The *Alcazaba*, Spain's largest Moorish fortress, was built in 955 under the Caliph of Córdoba. Expansion began after it was hit by a 16th-century earthquake. Its three curtain walls and ❊ towers climb up the hill in San Cristóbal. *April–mid-June Tue–Sat 9am–8pm, mid-June–mid-Sept 9am–3pm and 7pm–10pm, mid-Sept–March 9am–6pm, every Sun 9am–3pm | free admission for EU citizens*

CASA PUGA

It's worth the detour to Almería just to eat at this tapas bar. Their eclectic variety of mouthwatering tapas and extensive wine list are truly impressive. It's clearly the taste that has kept them going strong since 1870. *Closed Sun | C/ Jovellanos 7 | tel. 9 50 23 15 30 | www.barcasapuga.es | Budget–Moderate*

TABERNA NUESTRA TIERRA ✪

Tapas paired with the slow-food philosophy is a match made in heaven! Taste everything they have to offer, ranging from their *ajo colorao* (potato veggie ragout) served with smoked stockfish, to the pork cheeks smothered in Mozarabic sauce. *Daily | C/ Jovellanos 16 | tel. 6 79 89 74 32 | tabernanuestratierra.com | Moderate*

HOTEL CATEDRAL ALMERÍA

A 19th-century townhouse centrally located near the cathedral. Modern rooms and a small roof-top pool. *20 rooms | Plaza de la Catedral 8 | tel. 9 50 27 81 78 | www.hotelcatedral.net | Moderate*

TORRELUZ CENTRO

A two-star hotel located in the Old Town centre. The 24 rooms are furnished in an unobtrusive modern style. For more luxury and a pool, try the more expensive *Nuevo Torreluz* (*Moderate*). *Plaza de las Flores 8 | tel. 9 50 28 14 29 | www.torreluz. com | Budget*

INFORMATION

OFICINA DE TURISMO

Plaza de la Constitución | tel. 9 50 21 05 38 | www.turismodealmeria.org and *Parque Nicolás Salmerón | on the harbour promenade | tel. 9 50 17 52 20*

WHERE TO GO

DESIERTO DE TABERNAS
(155 D4–5) (*$\mathbb{M}$ N5*)

The Tabernas Desert: a grey-brown mountain landscape without the plants, sand or dust. Some prefer hiking through these barren yet exciting badlands. Others wear a cowboy hat and go by horse. With the backdrop being ideal for gun fights and grim faces, it's no wonder Charles Bronson and Clint Eastwood once acted here. Cowboy fans can sit in a saloon or watch a short western at *Oasys Mini-Hollywood* (*see website for showtimes | admission 22.50 euros | N 340 km 464 | www.oasysparquetematico. com*). There's also a western town, outdoor pool, zoo and theme park.

MOJÁCAR ≋ (155 F4) (*$\mathbb{M}$ O5*)

Offering a vast view over the sea, the white buildings on the hillside in Mojácar (pop. 6500, 90 km/55 mi northeast of Almeriá) have been there since the Moorish period. 2 km/1.2 mi from the Old Town, you'll find a slew of hotels, bars and restaurants on the coast. On the Costa del Sol, you'll find even more of the same and a 7 km/4.3 mi-long sandy beach. At the Roman restaurant *El Palacio (daily | C/ Lance 4 | tel. 6 52 65 34 35 | Moderate)*, Mediterranian and Moroccan cuisine is fused together. More elegant accommodation is found directly on the beach. Try the renovated *Parador de Mojácar (98 rooms | Playa de Mojácar | tel. 9 50 47 82 50 | www.parador.es | Moderate–Expensive)*. Information: *Oficina de Turismo (Plaza del Frontón | tel. 9 50 61 50 25 | www.mojacar.es)*

PARQUE NATURAL CABO DE GATA ★
(155 E–F 5–6) (*$\mathbb{M}$ N–06*)

A gravel road south of San José, 40 km/ 25 mi northeast of Almería, leads to perhaps the most beautiful beaches on Andalucía's Mediterranean coastline. The

A wildly romantic rocky coast east of Almería on the Cabo de Gata

secluded *Cala Los Amarillos,* a hidden beach where you can peacefully bathe in the nude, overlooks a volcanic landscape. A shifting sand dune separates the wide, crescent-shaped *Playa de los Genoveses.* The adjoining ● *Playa del Mónsul* and the *Cala de la Media Luna* are surrounded by unique rock formations. Beyond the decommissioned gold mines of Rodalquilar, you arrive at *Cortijo del Fraile*, where Federico García Lorca's play 'Blood Wedding' took place. *La Isleta del Moro* is a tiny fishing village only seen in dreams. Here you can enjoy fresh fish and paella at *Restaurante Isleta del Moro (open daily | right on the harbourside | tel. 9 50 38 97 13 | Budget–Moderate)* and have a wonderful view of the bay. Sophisticated Mediterranean cuisine is served at the charming *La Gallineta (closed Monday | El Pozo de Los Frailes | tel. 9 50 38 05 01 | Moderate–Expensive).* The INSIDER TIP *Cala del Plomo*, a secluded bay perfect for swimming, is reachable by foot along a lovely path from the beautiful town of Agua Amarga. One of the best places to stay in the park is the ecologically-run Casa Rural *La Joya de Cabo de Gata (Paraje La Joya/Agua Amarga | tel. 6 19 15 95 87 | www.lajoyadecabodegata.es | Moderate–Expensive).* Their three apartments are lovingly designed with a North African/Andalucían style and ideal for longer visits. The coast along the nature park is perfect for scuba diving and snorkelling. We recommend going to *Isub (C/ Babor 3 | tel. 9 50 38 00 04 | www.isubsanjose.com)*, located in San José. Their snorkelling course only costs 25 euros. The cliff *Arrecife de las Sirenas* is best explored by canoe. You can rent the vessel of your liking at *Cabo de Gata Activo (Playa de La Fabriquilla | tel. 6 33 41 83 83 | www.cabodegataactivo.com)* or have a tour guide paddle you through the southeast tip of Spain (25 euros and up). For

the park, take A 319. Get on Puerto de las Palomas, which will take you the 1290 m/ 4232 ft up into the mountains. From here, you can hike along the *Cerrada de Utrero,* the dam wall to the first reservoir in the Guadalquivir. Or hike for hours along the Río Borosa to the *Laguna de Valdeazores* or the *source of the Guadalquivir*, not far from Cazorla. The drive on the *Ruta Félix Rodríguez de la Fuente* is beautiful, circumferencing the reservoir Embalse del Tranco. The Rafael Zabaleta Museum in Quesada is ideal for art lovers.

SIGHTSEEING

Better leave the car in the car park under the Plaza Mercado and explore this mountain town on foot. From the *Plaza de Santa María*, which boasts a church ruin of the same name, you'll find a steep path towards the ☼ *Castillo de la Yedra*, a castle with a beautiful view.

more Information: *Oficina de Turismo in San José (Av. San José 27 | tel. 9 50 38 02 99 | www.cabodegata-nijar.com);* visitor centre for the natural park: *Centro de Visitantes de Las Amoladeras (Ctra. Cabo de Gata-Almería | tel. 9 50 16 04 35 | www. parquenatural.com)*

CAZORLA

(149 E3) *(ഗ L3)* ★ **This pretty mountain town is ideal for touring Spain's largest natural park: Parque Natural Sierras de Cazorla, Segura y Las Villas.** East of the province of Jaén, *Cazorla* (pop. 8000) is a little town surrounded by nature on the edge of Europe's second largest protected area: the Sierra de Cazorla. Covering 5542.5 sq mi of land, it boasts pine and holm oak forests intersected by rivers and reservoirs, mountains and steppes. To enter

FOOD & DRINK

MESÓN LEANDRO
This rustic restaurant specialises in grilling meat. *Daily | C/ La Hoz 3 | tel. 9 53 72 06 32 | www.mesonleandro.com | Budget–Moderate*

EL TRANCO
Outstanding taste and the perfect location. The outdoor terrace ☼ offers a spectacular view over the park's mountains and reservoir. *Daily | A 319, km 75 | Poblado del Tranco | tel. 9 53 00 22 76 | tranco.es | Moderate*

SPORTS & ACTVITIES

Sport enthusiasts will have plenty of amazing terrain to explore in this massive natural park. Whether it's kayaking, rafting or climbing, *Centro de Ocio &*

Turismo El Tranco (A 319, km 75 | Poblado del Tranco | tel. 9 53 00 22 76 | tranco.es) has all this and more. In Cazorla, *Turisnat (C/ José Martínez Falero 11 | tel. 9 53 72 13 51 | www.turisnat.es)* offers guided tours in Land Rovers that take you, e.g. to the source of the Guadalquivir. Rock climbing tours, mountain biking, canyoning and more can be booked at *Aventura Cazorla (A 319, km 16.5 | tel. 9 53 71 00 73 | www.aventuracazorla.com)*, located below the tower of La Iruela.

WHERE TO STAY

INSIDERTIP MOLINO LA FARRAGA

Near the Old Town and surrounded by nature is a unique guesthouse in a former watermill. *8 rooms | Camino de la Hoz | tel. 9 53 72 12 49 | www.molinola farraga.com | Budget*

PARADOR DE CAZORLA

This charming, hunting-lodge-style hotel is peacefully surrounded by the natural park and 24 km/15 mi outside of Cazorla. The pool offers a breathtaking panoramic view of the Sierra mountains. *36 rooms | tel. 9 53 72 70 75 | Moderate–Expensive*

SIERRA DE CAZORLA & SPA

Located on a mountain road above La Iruela, this hotel offers a large spa area. The outdoor and indoor pools are heated using biomass fuel (e.g. olive stones). *40 rooms | Ctra. de la Sierra 2 | La Iruela | tel. 9 53 72 00 15 | www.hotelsierrade cazorla.com | Moderate*

INFORMATION

OFICINA DE TURISMO

Plaza de Santa María | tel. 9 53 71 01 02 | www.cazorla.es. On the country road in the natural park: *Centro Interpretación de la Torre del Vinagre (Ctra. del Tranco |* *A 319, km 48.8 | tel. 9 53 71 30 17 | www. turismoencazorla.com)*

GRANADA

MAP INSIDE BACK COVER
(153 E3) *(K5)* **Saturday evening on the Carrera del Darro. The city's night owls take to the streets: language and university students, young Spaniards and foreigners. Tourists blend into the crowd, carried away by the happy jostling and magic of night-time Granada laughing and chatting; lovers and friends walk arm in arm from bar to bar.** Towering over the nightlife is the Alhambra, bathed in soft floodlighting. Opposite the fortress, the labyrinthine streets of the Albaicín, the old Moorish quarter, are silent. *Granada* (pop. 240,000) is a lively university city with an incredible history. During the 13th-century Reconquista, when Christians reconquered large parts of Spain, the Nasrid ruler Muhammad I made a pact with the Catholics that enabled him to found a Muslim kingdom in Granada. For 250 years following, Granada maintained a flourishing civilisation during the Dark Ages. With its construction beginning in 1238, the royal palace of Alhambra depicts

CITY WHERE TO START?
Plaza Nueva: Head for the Plaza Nueva. From here, it is just a short distance to the cathedral, Capilla Real and the narrow streets of the Albaicín district. The car park in Calle del Cristo de San Agustín (near Gran Vía) is very central. Or follow the car park routing system. Bus no. 33 starts at the station, with several stops along the Gran Vía.

Non-stop action: a street café in Albaicín, the Moorish Old Town of Granada

how strongly the Nasrids impacted the culture. However, the Christians' urge to conquer was ultimately more important than preserving the Nasrid culture. Consequently, on 2 January 1492, Boabdil, Spain's last Muslim ruler, gave Queen Isabella of Castile and Ferdinand of Aragón the key to the city.

Nonetheless, the Alhambra remains one of the most beautiful palaces in the world and is a beautiful memorial of the former Islamic Andalucía. Moreover, two-million-plus visitors come to marvel at this World Heritage Site each year. If you're travelling from the west into Granada, you'll have a magical view entering the city as it sits 685 m/2247 ft above sea level, below the (in spring) snow-covered peaks of the Sierra Nevada. It's best to avoid the route through the badly built suburbs, as it temporarily dampens the excitement. (For more detailed information, see the MARCO POLO guidebook 'Costa del Sol/Granada'.)

SIGHTSEEING

ALBAICÍN ★

The top of the mountain facing the Alhambra marks where Albaicín is located. Here is where the first settlement in Granada emerged. Although Iberians, Romans and Visigoths settled here from the 7th century onward, Albaicín didn't become a place of interest until the 11th century under Arabian rule. Over the years, the district has maintained its Moorish character, but none of the buildings, apart from the old town wall and its gates, date back to the Islamic era. In the 16th century following the expulsion of the Mosiscos (Muslims forced to convert to Christianity), many of the buildings fell into disrepair. These sites were used to build larger estates with walled gardens called *carmen*, for which Albaicín is famous today. Two such estates are open to visitors: the *Carmen Max Moreau (Tue–Sat 10.30am–1.30pm and 4pm–6pm | free admission | Camino nuevo de San Nicolás 12)* and the *Carmen Aljibe del Rey (guided tours Mon–Fri 12 noon | free admission | Plaza del Cristo de las Azucenas)*.

If you wish to aimlessly explore the district, take any narrow street or stairway weaving between the whitewashed buildings to be found. You'll find Muslim traditions and culture are still very much present here. In 2003, the *Mezquita Mayor*, Andalucía's first mosque, and where the gardens are free to visit, opened its doors. The liveliest squares are the *Placeta de San Miguel Bajo* and the shaded *Plaza Larga*. From the ● ☀ *Mirador de San Nicolás*, you can enjoy an unsurpassed view of the Alhambra. It's also

worth it to visit the *Palacio de Dar al-Horra (daily mid-Sept–April from 10am–5pm, May–mid-Sept 9.30am–2.30pm and 5pm–8.30pm | admission 5 euros | Callejón de las Monjas)* and the 11th-century Arabian baths in the *El Bañuelo (mid-Sept–April daily 10am–5pm, May–mid-Sept 9.30am–2.30pm and 5pm–8.30pm | admission 3.50 euros | Carrera del Darro 31)*. To the east is *Sacromonte* (the 'Holy Mountain'), which runs through the traditional district of the *gitanos* (the Romani people of Granada) with its town wall ruins and many cave dwellings.

ALHAMBRA ☆

The interior of the Alhambra ('The Red One') is like a treasure trove hidden behind mighty walls void of any ornamentation. These enclose a site divided into several totally different parts. At the western-most end are the remains of the Alcazaba, the citadel and administrative section. The ☀ *Torre de la Vela* boasts

Moorish décor: the Palacios Nazaríes in the Alhambra

views in two directions – to the north to Albaicín and to the south to the Sierra Nevada.

But the Alhambra's centrepiece is the *Palacios Nazaríes*: the palaces to the Nasrid rulers. The magnificence of the *Mexuar* (audience and council chamber) and the *Cuarto Dorado* (the Golden Room) hits you as soon as you cross the entrance. This beauty is then magnified upon entering the adjoining *Patio de los Arrayanes* (Court of the Myrtles) and the *Sala de los Embajadores* (Hall of the Ambassadors). It's said that the throne of the Nasrid kings once stood under the dream-like ceiling made of thousands of small cedar tiles.

From here, you enter the *Patio de los Leones* (Court of the Lions), the most photographed motif in the Alhambra; twelve stone lions stand in the middle of the courtyard in a circle beneath a marble basin. Equally breathtaking is the *Sala de los Abencerrajes* (Hall of the Abencerrajes). Its dome looks like a white sea of dripping honeycomb that solidified before it hit the ground. This image is then reflected in the twelve-sided basin below. The magic of the Nasrid culture fades upon entering the Renaissance building *Palacio de Carlos V (mid-Oct–March Tue–Sat 9am–6pm April–mid-June and mid-Sept–mid-Oct 9am–8pm, mid-June–mid-Sept 9am–3pm, all year on Sunday 10am–3pm | admission 1.50 euros)*. Carl V ordered it to be built inside the Alhambra, and its construction began in 1526. Although square, the building displays a circular patio within and houses the Museum of Fine Arts, in which 15th–20th-century works are displayed in eight halls. Also located in the Alhambra is the hotel *Parador de Granada*. Although the rooms are usually booked, you can cool down in their quiet bar. Before you leave, be sure to visit the ☘ blossoming gardens around the *Generalife*, a summer palace just beyond the Alhambra.

It's best to buy your ticket to the Alhambra in advance to avoid waiting in line just to find the maximum number of tickets sold has been reached (6600 a day). Do this by going online at *www.alhambra-tickets.es*. You'll be able to pick up your tickets at the machines outside of the enterance to the Alhambra or at one of the *Servicaixa* cash machines located throughout Andalucía. Once in Spain, you can also book your tickets at any Caixa Bank. Again, same-day tickets are available at the cash desk at the Alhambra entrance, but only until they've sold their limit on tickets. You may only enter the Palacios Nazaríes at the time printed on your ticket, and morning visitors must leave the Alhambra by 2pm. Since the *Granada Card (free admission to all main attractions and use of public transport | 37 euros)* has its own allotment of tickets, it may be worth it to buy the ticket. *April–mid-Oct daily 8.30am–8pm, evening visits to the Palacios Nazaríes Tue–Sat 10pm–11.30pm, mid-Oct–March daily 8.30am–6pm, evening visits Fri/Sat 8pm–9.30pm | complete admission 14 euros, night visit 8 euros, Gardens 7 euros | www.alhambra-patronato.es, www.alham bradegranada.org*

CATHEDRAL AND LOWER CITY AREA

Completely surrounded by other buildings, the Renaissance cathedral *Santa María de la Encarnación (Mon–Sat 10am–6.30pm, Sun 3pm–6pm | admission 5 euros | catedraldegranada.com)* is mostly the work of architect Diego de Siloé. Although the exterior may seem unimpressive, just wait until you get inside. The *Capilla Mayor* is remarkable: 22 m/ 72 ft in diameter and 45 m/148 ft high. Next to the cathedral is the *Capilla Real (Mon–Sat 10.15am–18.30pm, Sun 11am–*

18.30pm | admission 5 euros | C/ Oficios 3 | www.capillarealgranada.com), the Royal Chapel where the Catholic monarchs Isabella of Castile and Ferdinand of Aragón have been buried since 1521. Next to their tomb also rests their daughter Joanna the Mad and her husband Philip the Handsome. In the adjoining room is Isabella's personal collection of 15th-century paintings, including masterpieces by Rogier van der Weyden and Sandro Botticelli. *Alcaicería* is further south and filled with narrow streets. During the Moorish era, silk and cloth sellers had their shops here. Today, you'll find everything the souvenir industry has to offer. At the heart of the bustling city centre is the *Plaza Bib-Rambla* with its many cafés. Cardinal Cisneros, Isabella's Father Confessor, masterminded the burning of books here in 1499 during which the majority of Arabian writings in Al-Andalus were lost. The *Corral del Carbón (C/ Carrera Pineda)* is the oldest Arabian structure in Granada. The former 'caravanserai' (trading inn) was later used as a theatre and coal store – which gave it its present name. East of the city, you'll find *Realejo,* the city's former Jewish neighbourhood, which has been increasingly growing in popularity. Here you can take a walk along the southern side of the Alhambra or visit one of the lively bars or restaurants in *Campo del Príncipe.*

MONASTERIO DE LA CARTUJA
The building of this charterhouse monastery (located a bit north, outside the centre) started in 1514 and wasn't completed until 1794. It is an exceptional example of the exuberant Spanish Baroque style. *Daily 10am–8pm | admission 5 euros | Paseo de la Cartuja*

FOOD & DRINK

ALACENA DE LAS MONJAS
This restaurant offers both tapas and gourmet dishes. One of the dining areas is located in a 15th-century vault cellar. *Closed Mon | Plaza del Padre Suárez 5 |*

THE BIG SCREEN IN THE FLESH

Osuna is by no means the centre of the world, yet avid readers of 'Game of Thrones' have probably heard of the palaces here. Perhaps they've even stayed the night in the beautiful Hotel Palacio Marqués de la Gomera. However, with the TV series now filming some of the 5th season here, Osuna is no longer an insider among readers.

Today, there are thousands of people who want to see the bullring where a 17-minute fighting scene was shot and the hotel where their beloved hollywood stars stayed. Geographical locations seen on-screen are becoming more popular to visit than those described in literature. Although the experience of seeing the place depicted in literary or cinematic fiction is the same, the places seen on-screen mirror the visual memories and emotions perfectly. This holds true whether you're standing in Osuna, on the Playa del Mónsul on the Cabo de Gata ('Indiana Jones and the Last Crusade') or in the Tabernas Desert (e.g. '2001: A Space Odyssey', 'The Good, the Bad and the Ugly'). In short, an augemented reality is created.

Late Gothic grandeur: the marble grave of the 'Catholic Monarchs' in the Capilla Real

tel. 9 58 22 95 19 | alacenadelasmonjas. com | *Expensive*

BODEGAS CASTAÑEDA

A bar straight out of a picture-book – old wine barrels, a wooden drinks bar, a bull's head and delicious tapas. *Daily | C/ Almireceros 1 | tel. 9 58 21 54 64 | Budget– Moderate*

LOS DIAMANTES

Neon lighting and no hip design elements, yet there are few tapas bars in Granada that have as much atmosphere as here. Good, generous helpings. Other tapas bars can be found in the Calle Navas. *Daily | C/ Navas 28 | tel. 9 58 22 70 70 | www.barlosdiamantes.com | Budget*

MIRADOR DE MORAYMA ⊚

Masterfully placed in an old palacio in Albaicín, this restaurant has a beautiful interior with antique furnishings. The terrace ⊱ offers a wonderful view of the Alhambra. Organic wine from its own vineyards. *Closed Sun evening | C/ Pianista García Carrillo 2 | tel. 9 58 22 82 90 | Moderate–Expensive*

INSIDER TIP ▶ TABERNA LA TANA

Small as this tapas bar may be, the choice of excellent wines is huge and the little snacks are a real treat. *Daily | Placeta del Agua 3 | tel. 9 58 22 52 48 | www. tabernalatana.com | Budget–Moderate*

SHOPPING

Between the cathedral and the Plaza Bib-Rambla, you'll find the buildings of the *Alcaicería*. Hemmed in by other souvenir shops, this old market now specialises in jewellery and crafted items for tourist trade. The approach to the Alhambra in the *Cuesta de Gomérez* presents a similar picture. A bazaar-like atmosphere with tea rooms, restaurants and shops can be found in the streets *Calderería Nueva* and *Calderería Vieja*, located at the foot of the

Albaicín. Hand-made ceramics, marquetry and guitar making – *e.g. Miguel Ángel Bellido (C/ Navas 22)* and *Guitarrería Gil de Avalle (Plaza del Realejo 15)* – have a long tradition in Granada. If you'd like to taste and see local culinary specialities, the *Mercado de San Agustín (Plaza de San Agustín)* is definitely the place to go.

ENTERTAINMENT

At weekends, there is always a lot going on around the *Plaza Nueva* and in the *Calle Elvira* and *Carrera del Darro*, where there are several tapas and cocktail bars and the disco club *Granada 10 (C/ Cárcel Baja 10)*. The dance club *Camborio* is on the road to the *gitano* district Sacromonte. The best-known and largest nightclub is *Mae West (C/ Arabial/Centro Comercial Neptuno)*, south of the city centre.

LOW BUDGET

FLAMENCO

The flamenco restaurants in Granada are located in the caves of Sacromonte, behind the Albaicín. Included in the ticket price, you can usually decide if you'd like a free drink or supper during the show. You may also request to be picked up at your hotel. Recommended locations are, e.g. the *Cueva La Rocío (daily 9pm, 10pm, 11pm | tickets start at 20 euros | Camino del Sacromonte 70 | tel. 9 58 22 71 29 | cuevalarocio.es)* and the *Cueva Venta El Gallo (daily starting at 7.30pm | tickets start at 26 euros | Barranco de los Negros 5 | tel. 9 58 22 84 76 | ventael gallo.com)*.

WHERE TO STAY

CASA BOMBO

A lovely guest house with seven rooms, some of which have a view of the Alhambra, including INSIDER TIP the Tower Room, with a balcony. Not all of the rooms have their own washroom, but there's a small pool on the public terrace where you can relax under the sun and dream. *C/ Aljibe de Trillo 22 | tel. 9 58 29 06 35 | casabombo.com | Budget*

CASA 1800

The city palace Los Migueletes is located at the foot of the Albaicín. Its interior exudes a Baroque opulence with a plethora of gold-leaf curlicues. *25 rooms | C/ Benalúa 11 | tel. 9 58 21 07 00 | www.hotelcasa1800granada.com | Expensive*

INSIDER TIP GAR-ANAT

In this historical town palace, Mika Murakami has transformd some of the rooms into poetic stages. Those who like such things will be full of enthusiasm for this hotel. *15 rooms | Placeta de los Peregrinos 1 | tel. 9 58 22 55 28 | hotelgaranat.com | Moderate–Expensive*

The Castillo San Miguel is the Moorish fortress of Almuñécar

EL LADRÓN DE AGUA

This small hotel is located in a beautiful, 16th-century town palace along the tiny Darro River below the Albaicín. The lobby boasts an artistic library and a changing art exhibition. *15 roooms | Carrera del Darro 13 | tel. 9 58 21 50 40 | www.ladron deagua.com | Expensive*

MACÍA PLAZA

It's hard to get more central than this! The hotel's location is perfect for touring the main attractions, including the Alhambra, Albaicín and the cathedral. The rooms are offered at a fair price despite the hotel's centrality, especially during the low season. *44 rooms | Plaza Nueva 5 | Tel. 9 58 28 58 06 | www.macia plaza.com | Moderate*

INFORMATION

OFICINA DE TURISMO

Plaza del Carmen 9 | Tel. 9 58 24 82 80 | www.granadatur.com; other information offices in the Alhambra and on the *C/ Santa Ana 2 (directly next to the Plaza Nueva)*

WHERE TO GO

ALMUÑÉCAR (153 E5) *(𝄞 K6)*

This popular seaside resort (pop. 28,000) is 80 km/49 mi south of Granada on the Costa Tropical – the main coastline of the province of Granada. The long, clean, pebbly beaches have been rather spoilt by new buildings, but the Old Town is lovely for a stroll. The Moorish fortress *Castillo de San Miguel (Tue–Sat 10am– 1.30pm, 5pm–7.30pm, Sun 10.30–1pm | admission 2.35 euros)* is situated above the town. The neighbouring bay of *La Herradura* is not only a meeting place for wind and kite surfers. Located directly on the beach, at *Windsurf La Herradura (tel. 6 75 98 33 24 | windsurflaherradura.com)* you can rent a kayak, rent a board for stand-up paddling or take a surfing course. If you're hungry, head over to the Calle Manila in the centre; here you'll find plenty of tapas bars. Delicious fish and seafood can also be had at *Restaurante Ana María (daily | Paseo San Cristóbal 2 | tel. 9 58 63 26 38 | www.restaurantean amaria.com | Budget–Moderate)*, located on the beach promenade of San Cristóbal. Almuñécar's most beautiful hotel is the *Casablanca (35 rooms | Plaza San Cristóbal 4 | tel. 9 58 63 55 75 | www.hotel casablancaalmunecar.com | Budget)*. Information: *Oficina de Turismo (Av. de Europa 12 | Palacete de la Najarra | Tel. 9 58 63 11 25 | www.turismoalmunecar.es)*

ALPUJARRAS ★ (153 F4) (*Ø K6*)

Dozens of little villages from the Moorish period are hidden in the barren mountains on the southern slope of the Sierra Nevada. Moroccan settlers brought the skills they learned in the Atlas Mountains with them, cutting terraces, planting and irrigating fields and building architecture unique to Andalucía. The flat slate roofs are covered with *launa*, a black clay that absorbs rainwater. It's well worth the excursion to visit the ▵ *Valle de Poqueira* and the three villages *Pampaneira*, *Bubión* and *Capileira* in the valley. Vegan cuisine is served at a cosy restaurant in Capileira called *La Tapa (daily | C/ Cubo 6 | tel. 6 18 30 70 30 | Budget–Moderate)*. The lovely hotel in the city is *Rural Finca Los Llanos (40 rooms | Ctra. Sierra Nevada | tel. 9 58 76 30 71 | hotel fincalosllanos.com | Budget)*. Information in Pampaneira: *Centro de Visitantes (Plaza Libertad | tel. 9 58 76 31 27)*. 1480 m/ 4856 ft up the mountain and 25 km/ 15 mi further east is the village of *Trevélez*. Their world-renowned ham is some of the best you can find in Spain.

GUADIX (153 F3) (*Ø L5*)

About 60 km/37 mi east of Granada is *Guadix* (pop. 19,000). House façades stick to the sides of cliffs; their chimneys shoot out of the soil. These are cave dwellings. 1300 of them are scattered around the district of Santiago here. Even in pre-Roman times, people dug into the earth here. Today, the caves are comfortably equipped. It's also worth it to see the 15th-century *cathedral*. Diego de Siloé designed this Renaissance building – the same architect made famous for the marvellous Granada Cathedral. There is a really beautiful and affordable hotel in the middle of the centre called INSIDER TIP ▸ *Abentofail (30 rooms | C/ Abentofail 8 | tel. 9 58 66 92 81 | www. hotelabentofail.com | Budget–Moderate)* that also has an incredible restaurant. Set against the snow-covered peaks of the Sierra Nevada is the Renaissance castle of *La Calahorra*, with its four round towers, 15 km/9.3 mi further to the east *(Wed 10am–1pm, 4pm–6pm)*. Information: *Oficina de Turismo (Plaza de la Constitución 15 | tel. 9 58 66 28 04 | www.guadix.es)*

SALOBREÑA (153 E5) (*Ø K6*)

A good 60 km/37 mi south of Granada, there's a white village (pop. 13,000) sitting on a rocky prominence on the Costa Tropical. Steep, narrow streets wind their way up the mountainside between houses landscaped with flowers to reach an ▵ Arab *Castillo* from the 13th century. The village is surrounded by sugarcane plantations. However, the plain that stretches as far as the beach is losing its charm with every new hotel and apartment block. For surprisingly good, highquality cuisine, go to INSIDER TIP ▸ *Aráis (daily | C/ Granada 11 | tel. 9 58 61 17 38 | Moderate)*. The restaurant turns into a well frequented bar at night. *Hostal Jayma (13 rooms | C/ Cristo 24 | tel. 9 58 61 02 31 | www.hostaljayma.com | Budget)* is a well maintained hostel just below the Old Town. Information: *Oficina de Turismo (Plaza Goya | tel. 9 58 61 03 14 | turismosalobrena.com)*

SIERRA NEVADA (153 E–F4) (*Ø K5*)

The highest mountains on the Spanish mainland are the *Mulhacén* (3481 m/

11,420 ft) and the *Pico de Veleta* (3398 m/11,148 ft). In this snowy range near Granada, you'll find Europe's most southern skiing slopes and Spain's largest national park. These 332 sq mi are surrounded by another Natural Park where the ibex and eagle roam. Given the season and your mood, there are many things you can do outside of these protected areas, like skiing, mountain biking, hiking, horseback riding, rock climbing and off-road tours. Information and maps in the national park: *Centro de Visitantes El Donajo (A 395 to Pradollano, at km 23 | tel. 9 58 34 06 25 | www.sierra nevada.es, www.nevadensis.com)*.

JAÉN

(148 B4) (*ℳ J3*) **This provincial capital (pop. 115,000) is located on a hill below the towering Sierra de la Pandera and forms a gateway to Andalucía.**

Towering above the labyrinthine, narrow streets of the markedly Arabian Old Town is the *Renaissance Catedral Asunción de la Virgen (daily | 10am–2pm and 5pm–8pm, in winter 10am–2pm and 4pm–7pm | admission 5 euros)*. The vaulted Arabian baths from the 11th century are beneath the *Palacio Villardompardo (Tue–Sat 9am–10pm, Sun 9am–3pm | free admission for EU citizens)*. The top attraction in the seldom-visited Old Town is the palace next to the cathedral, which houses both a *folk museum* and a *museum for naïve art*. The paintings are moving and remarkable to see. At the museum's café, you can enjoy a panoramic view of the Old Town and the olive groves from their ☀ viewing deck. The same view can also be gloriously seen from the tower ☀ *Castillo de Santa Catalina, (Oct–June Mon–Sat 10am–6pm, July–Sept 10am–2pm and 5pm–9pm, Sun 10am–*

Capileira: a village in the Alpujarras on the southern slope of the Sierra Nevada

JAÉN

WHERE TO START?

Plaza de la Constitución: The upper part of Jaén and its cathedral are both fascinating. From here, you can explore the Old Town and the Palacio de Villardompardo. The underground car park near the Plaza de la Constitución is easy to access. Bus routes 1 and 2 link, e.g. the provincial museum with the Plaza de la Constitución.

3pm | admission 3.50 euros). From here, you can see row upon row of trees threading through the olive groves. There's also a small exhibition inside the tower explaining how farm life was during the Middle Ages in Spain.

FOOD & DRINK

The *Plaza del Posito* is a pleasant square with bars and cafés. Tapas bars such as the rustic *La Manchega (C/ Bernardo López 8)* can be found on and around the *Calle Cerón*.

PANACEITE

Above the Plaza del Posito, you'll find the the new favourite restaurant of the Jaén people: the *Panaceite*. Whether it's breakfast, lunch or dinner, their menu has you covered. The dishes are beautifully prepared and served with kindness. And the house vermouth is so palatable. *Daily | C/ Bernabé Soriano 1 | tel. 9 53 24 06 30 | Moderate*

WHERE TO STAY

PARADOR DE JAÉN ⚘

From a private balcony, the rooms provide you with a phenomenal view of the Castillo de Santa Catalina. Meals are served in a spacious knights' hall. The bar boasts an enormous fireplace, and their rustic parlour will take you back to the Middle Ages. *45 rooms | tel. 9 53 23 00 00 | www.parador.es | Expensive*

INFORMATION

OFICINA DE TURISMO

C/ Ramón y Cajal 1 | tel. 9 53 19 04 55 | www.turjaen.org, www.promojaen.es

WHERE TO GO

BAEZA AND ÚBEDA ★
(148–149 C–D3) *(⌒ K3)*

Spain's two most beautiful Renaissance towns are 46 km/29 mi and 54 km/33.5 mi northeast of Jaén, and both of them have been declared Unesco World Heritage Sites. In *Baeza* (pop. 17,000), visitors find themselves in a world like no other, surrounded by the Santa Cruz church and Santa María plaza. Built between the 15th and 17th centuries, the façade of the *Palacio de Jabalquinto* is embellished with décor in Isabelline Gothic style. Diagonally opposite, the late Romanesque church of *Santa Cruz* provides a stark contrast. The construction of the *Antigua Universidad* ended in 1542. There are plenty of beautiful photo ops on the *Plaza de Santa María*, which boasts a picturesque 16th-century cathedral, the *Seminario de San Felipe Neri* (now an international university) and the beautiful *Casas Consistoriales*. An equally picture-perfect backdrop can be found on the *Plaza del Pópulo*, with its Roman lion sculptures, known as the *Fuente de Leones*. The square is surrounded by the *Antigua Carnicería*, a former abattoir presenting a brilliant façade.

The *Plaza de la Constitución* feels like the living room of the city. Here you'll find many bars and restaurants representing

Spanish culture. If you're lucky to get a table, amazing tapas and urban cuisine can be had at INSIDER TIP *La Barbería (closed Mon/Tue | C/ Conde Romanones 11 |* *Reales Alcázares*, the granary *Antiguo Pósito*, the *Capilla del Salvador*, with its Renaissance façade, and the *Palacio del Deán Ortega*, which now houses the

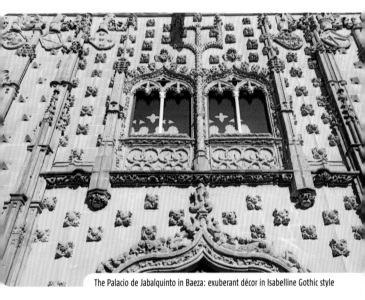

The Palacio de Jabalquinto in Baeza: exuberant décor in Isabelline Gothic style

tel. 6 71 07 85 09 | Moderate). You can taste the best olive oil in the area at INSIDER TIP *Casa de Aceite (Paseo de la Constitución 9)* and stay the night in the charming hotel called *Puerta de la Luna (24 rooms | C/ Canónigo Melgares Raya | tel. 9 53 74 70 19 | www.hotelpuertadela luna.com | Budget–Expensive)*. The hotel bar *Paco's* has great tapas and drinks that even the people from Baeza come to enjoy. Information: *Oficina de Turismo | Plaza del Pópulo | tel. 9 53 77 99 82 | www.jaenparaisointerior.es*. Once in *Úbeda* (pop. 36,000), follow the signs to the Parador. Eventually, you'll reach the *Plaza Vázquez de Molina*, surrounded by magnificent 16th-century architecture, including the *Palacio de las Cadenas*, the church *Santa María de los*

Parador *(tel. 9 53 75 03 45 | www.para dor.es | Moderate–Expensive)*. If you'd like to stay here, ask for INSIDER TIP room no. 112! It's the corner room opposite the main entrance to the *Capilla del Salvador*. Pass the chapel and the Hospital del Salvador and you'll reach the ● ⚜ *Plaza Santa Lucía*. From here, you'll have a view over the olive groves.

Lovely ceramics are sold at the pottery *Alfarería Tito (Plaza del Ayuntamiento 12)*. Offering affordable and delicious cuisine, the oddest restaurant in the city is *Cantina La Estación (closed Tue evening and Wed | Cuesta Rodadera 1 | tel. 6 87 77 72 30 | Moderate)*, with its interior resembling that of a dining car's. Information: *Oficina de Turismo | Plaza de Andalucía 5 | tel. 9 53 77 92 04 | turismodeubeda.com*

THE SOUTH

Each year, the southern sun, sand and sea attract millions of visitors worldwide as they flock to the beaches on the Costa de la Luz between Nerja and Sanlúcar de Barrameda and on the Costa del Sol (for more information, see the MARCO POLO guidebook 'Costa del Sol').

The real attraction of the Andalucían south, however, covers the provinces of Cádiz and Málaga and lies inland from the rows of huge tourist hotels. The enchanting 'White Towns' in the Sierra de Grazalema epitomise the dream of the Moorish south. Only 'romantic Ronda' on the split rocky plateau can hold its own in the face of such untamed beauty. Many of the places have 'de la Frontera' added to their name as a reminder of the Reconquista period, when the Christians re-

gained control and the borders between Catholic and Moorish Spain were constantly changing in the hard fought-over south. Under the rule of the Almohad dynasty, enormous fortress complexes, Arabian baths and small mosques were built during this period.

CÁDIZ

(150 A4) (*C7*) **In the evenings on the Campo del Sur and on the Alameda de Apodaca, the people in ★ Cádiz (pop. 120,000) enjoy breathing in the salty air and soaking in the last rays of sun as it sets over the sea.**

Europe's oldest city (founded by the Phoenicians in the 11th century BC) is

Escape from the concrete jungle to one of the many beautiful beaches and explore the magical white villages further inland

WHERE TO START?

To tour the city, start at the walled-in Old Town of **Paseo de Canalejas**. In a round pavillion, you'll find the tourist information centre. Below the green landscaping is an underground car park. The cathedral is not much further from here. To reach the outskirts of the Old Town, take the inner-city bus or ferry from Puerto de Santa María.

flanked by the Atlantic on three sides. Apart from the small beach in the west, a city wall separates the land and ocean. Within the city wall, Baroque townhouses, some with tall lookout towers, dominate the scene. Merchants used to keep watch here to see their ships approaching the harbour. In 1717, Cádiz was granted a monopoly to trade with Latin America, which had previously brought considerable wealth to Seville. Known for its many tiny squares, this lovely city is home to the *Gaditanos*, the Cádiz people.

Lost in the Old Town of Cádiz? The domed cathedral is a good point of reference

CATEDRAL

When gleaming in the sun, the cathedral sparkles of sandstone, jasper and marble décor (1722–1838, with Baroque and neo-Classical elements). One of Spain's most important 20th-century composers, Manuel de Falla (1876–1946), was born in Cádiz and is buried in the cathedral's crypt. The admission fee to the cathedral includes entry to the *Museo de la Catedral (Mon–Sat 10am–4pm)*, located in the Casa de Contaduría on the Plaza Fray Félix. You may also enter the ☀️ *Torre del Reloj,* a clock tower offering a magnificent view over the city. *Mon–Sat 10am–7pm, Sun 2pm–7pm | admission 5 euros*

MUSEO DE CÁDIZ ●

This museum brings archaeology and art under one roof. Its treasures include two sarcophaguses from the Phoenician period (5th century BC), a statue of Emperor Trajan found in a Roman settlement and artworks from the 16th–20th centuries. The INSIDER TIP collection of paintings by Zurbarán is also one of a kind. The exceptional talent of this spiritually-minded Baroque artist is particularly apparent in his depiction of saints ('The Ecstasy of St Bruno', 'The Vision of St Francis of Assisi'). *Mid-June–mid-Sept Tue–Sun 10am–5pm, mid-Sept–mid-June Tue–Sat 10am–8.30pm, Sun 10am–5pm | free admission for EU-citizens | Plaza de Mina*

ORATORIO DE SAN FELIPE NERI

A beautiful Baroque church in Andalucía, its elliptical floor is illuminated by the natural light shining through the cupola. This national landmark is where the *Cortes* (the Spanish parliament) assembled in 1811/12 to draw up Spain's first liberal constitution. The monument on the Plaza España depicts a failed democracy. *Tue–Fri 10.30am–2pm and 4.30pm–8pm (July/Aug 5.30pm–8.30pm), Sat 10.30am–2pm, Sun 10am–1pm | admission 3 euros | C/ San José 38*

TORRE TAVIRA

A table-like screen glows in a dark room. You believe it's just an image of the city until you see people moving around in it. Although impressive, the video isn't created using magic or virtual reality. This camera, the camera obscura, was invented in the 10th-century by the Arab astronomer Abu Ali al-Hasan. *Daily 10am–6pm, May–Sept until 8pm | admissiion 6 euros | C/ Marqués del Real Tesoro 10 | www.torretavira.com*

FOOD & DRINK

Several tapas restaurants with outdoor terraces are located in the Calle Plocia. Two of many good recommendations are *El Aljibe* and *La Cepa Gallega*.

LA CANDELA

A traditional tapas bar with charming retro flair, serving, e.g. fish and chips, ceviche and grilled octopus. Most international cuisine comes from the sea. *Daily | C/ Feduchy 3 | tel. 9 56 22 18 22 | Budget–Moderate*

FREIDURÍA LAS FLORES

This restaurant combines the word *freiduría*, a snack bar in the south of Andalucía, with *Las Flores,* a true institution in Cádiz. Instead of bangers and mash, they serve fish and seafood. Tasty (but greasy!). *Daily / Plaza de las Flores | Budget*

MESÓN CUMBRES MAYORES

The legs of ham hanging from the ceiling are not a decoration; it's what's for dinner! The meat and grilled food are all the rage at this well-known tapas restaurant. *Daily | C/ Zorrilla 4 | Tel. 9 56 21 32 70 | www.mesoncumbresmayores.com | Moderate*

SHOPPING

Next to the Plaza de las Flores with its flower market, you'll find the *Mercado Central*, a neo-Classical market building

MARCO POLO HIGHLIGHTS

★ Cádiz
A lively Old Town with smooth, sandy beaches → p. 76

★ Sherry Bodegas
The cathedrals of wine, the nectar in Jerez de la Frontera → p. 84

★ Museo Picasso Málaga
A collection donated by Picasso's family; Málaga gives tribute → p. 88

★ Ronda
A city in balance → p. 95

★ Tarifa
A Southern European city and beloved holiday spot for surfers → p. 98

★ The White Towns
Arcos, Grazalema and Zahara: glowing pearls between powerful mountains → p. 101

★ Garganta del Chorro
A hair-raising trail through a spectacular canyon on the Caminito del Rey → p. 91

★ El Torcal
A science-fiction landscape with wild karst formations → p. 91

★ Centre Pompidou Málaga
The centre for contemporary art below a colourful cube on the port promenade → p. 88

with a tempting range of culinary delicacies. Caught on the Costa de la Luz, the tuna here is especially good; buy it deep-frozen or pickled at *Gadira (C/ Plocia 8)*.

BEACHES

West of the Old Town, the *Playa de la Caleta* is just 450 m/1476 ft long. On the south side of the strip is the larger *Playa de la Victoria* (2.5 km/1.5 mi), which connects Cádiz with the rest of Andalucía.

SPORTS & ACTIVITIES

Ferries to *El Puerto de Santa María (duration 30 minutes, return ticket 5.30 euros | www.cmtbc.es)* depart from the harbour several times a day. The best way to reach the Old Town or the southern sandy beaches is by bike. At *Urban Bike Cádiz (C/ Marqués de Valdeíñigo 4 | tel. 6 64 08 13 81 | www.urbanbikecadiz. es),* you can rent a bike for 14 euros a day.

WHERE TO STAY

INSIDER TIP **ARGANTONIO**

This charming little hotel in the Old Town of Cádiz gets a good number of positive reviews on online travel forums, and rightly so! Granted, the rooms are a bit small, but they're all tastefully and comfortably furnished. The location is perfect, and the value is good for your money. *15 rooms | C/ Argantonio 3 | tel. 9 56 21 16 40 | www.hotelargantonio.com | Moderate*

PARADOR DE CÁDIZ 🌿

The hotels of the Parador chain are often located in old palaces, monestaries and castles. The Parador in Cádiz, however, was built in the 1970s and has an elegantly modern design. The hotel also offers a beautiful pool with a great view overlooking the sea. *149 rooms | Av. Duque de Nájera 9 | tel. 9 56 22 69 05 | www.parador.es | Expensive*

Ferns, hand fans and a cool patio in Conil

INFORMATION

OFICINA MUNICIPAL DE TURISMO
Paseo de Canalejas | tel. 9 56 24 10 01 | www.cadizturismo.com

CONIL DE LA FRONTERA

(150 B5) *(ᗰ D7)* **The traffic squeezes through the Puerta de la Villa on the Plaza de España and past the guests sitting outside the cafés.**

Located on the Costa de la Luz Conil (pop. 22,500), Conil was once filled with backpackers and language school students. Today, it has long since been discovered by tour operators and is slowly trying to become more up-market. The locals carry on their business as usual, adding to the attraction of the place. The best thing here are the beaches. To the west, you'll find Calas del Cabo de Roche, with its small sandy coves nested between tall, steep cliffs. A stone's throw away is a giant beach more than 250 m/820 ft wide. It runs east all the way to El Palmar, a settlement where Sevillians love surfing.

FOOD & DRINK

FRANCISCO FONTANILLA
A beautifully situated and popular beach restaurant specialising in seafood. *Daily in July/Aug, otherwise closed on Tue | Playa de la Fontanilla | tel. 9 56 44 08 02 | Moderate*

SPORTS & ACTIVITIES

Tours on horseback can be booked at *Centro Hípico Pinares y Mar (Ctra. Fuente del Gallo, Cañada El Rosal | tel. 9 56*

44 30 60 | mobile 6 49 98 62 75 | www. picaderopacheco.com). Many surfers love riding the swells of the El Palmar, a long, sandy beach southeast of Conil.

WHERE TO STAY

CASA ALBORADA
The large hotels in Conil usually only book their rooms at a fixed rate. Not at this hostel! Boasting Azulejo-style walls and a landscaped patio, the spirit of Andalucía is certainly felt here. You're welcome to sunbathe on the roof, but they don't have a pool. *11 rooms | C/ General Gabino Aranda 5 | tel. 9 56 44 39 11 | www.alboradaconil.com | Budget*

EL PÁJARO VERDE
A simple but beautifully situated guesthouse right on the beach of El Palmar. 🌐 Restaurant serving organic food. *8 rooms | El Palmar | tel. 6 36 41 67 21 | www.el pajaroverde.com | Budget*

INFORMATION

OFICINA DE TURISMO
C/ Ctra. 1 | Tel. 9 56 44 05 01 | turismo. conil.org

WHERE TO GO

MEDINA SIDONIA, BENALUP AND THE LOS ALCORNOCALES NATURAL PARK
The Plaza de la Iglesia Mayor is 40 km/ 25 mi northeast of Conil and sits at the top of *Medina Sidonia* **(150 B–C4)** *(ᗰ D7)* (pop. 12,000). Steep, narrow streets lead the way, but the view is worth it. Take the steps up the ⚞ church tower of the *Iglesia de Santa María La Coronada (Feb–mid-Sept daily 11am–2pm and 5pm–8pm, otherwise open for Mass | admission 2.50 euros, combined ticket incl. the Roman excavations 4 euros)*

from the 14th–17th centuries. From the top, you'll see the Atlantic, the Sierra de Grazalema and many white villages appearing like snow on the sides of mountains. A well-preserved section of Roman road can also be visited called the *Calzada Romana*. It runs up to 4 m/13 ft below the Calle Alamo. Also worth seeing is the canalisation system used during Antiquity, the *Conjunto Arqueológico Romano (Tue–Sun 10am–2pm, 4pm–6pm | admission 3.10 euros, combined ticket with the Iglesia de Santa María La Coronada 4 euros | C/ Ortega)*. Possibly Andalucía's oldest church is from the 7th century and southwest of the town. *El Castillo (daily | C/ Ducado de Medina Sidonia 3 | tel. 9 56 41 08 23 | Moderate)* serves delicious, regional cuisine. Their veranda offers a beautiful view. *Information: Oficina de Turismo (C/ San Juan | tel. 9 56 41 24 04 | medinasidonia.com)*

20 km/12.4 mi further southeast over the green hilly countryside is *Benalup-Casas Viejas* (150 C5) *(E7)*. In 1933, anarchists instigated a revolution here, which cost them their lives. Embodying the revolutionary energy surrounding these Bohemian Spanish liberals, the hotel INSIDER TIP *Utopia (16 rooms | C/ Dr. Rafael Bernal 32 | tel. 9 56 41 95 32 | www.hotelutopia.es | Budget–Moderate)* has captured the spirit of the 1930s. Concerts and shows are regularly held in the restaurant *La Fonda*.

A bit further north is the *Los Alcornocales Natural Park* (150–151 C–D 4–5) *(E6–8)*, with its lakes and cork oak forests. Still a well-kept secret, the park's forest trails and terrain are used by mountain bikers, and many of the trails have been developed by the *Centro BTT Alcornocales (tel. 9 56 62 08 14 | www.centrobttalcornocales.com)*.

A sea of freshly debarked holm oaks at Los Alcornocales Natural Park

INSIDERTIP **A SCULPTURE GARDEN: FUNDACIÓN NMAC MONTENMEDIO** (150 C5) (*m D8*)

Sculptures by international artists such as Marina Abramović, Santiago Sierra and James Turrell are on display in a grove of pine trees, cork oaks and olive trees. An impressive museum that weaves art with nature. *Feb–May and Oct/Nov Tue–Sun 10am–2pm and 4pm–6.30pm, June and Sept 10am–2pm and 4pm–8pm, Jul/Aug 10am–2pm and 5pm–9pm, Dec/Jan 10am–2pm | admission 5 euros | on the N 340, km 42.5 between Tarifa and Vejer | www.fundacionnmac.org*

VEJER DE LA FRONTERA AND BARBATE
● (150 B5) (*m D7*)

16 km/10 mi southeast of Conil is *Vejer de la Frontera* (pop. 13,000). Called Andalucía's 'white beauty', the town sits on a 200 m/656 ft-high hill and boasts patios full of flowers, *azulejos* and four frogs that spout water on the Plaza de España with its many palm trees. The Moorish *Castillo de Vejer* is in the middle of the town. In the bistro market place *Mercado de San Francisco (C/ Juan Relinque)*, snacks and tapas are served (e.g. tacos, empanadas, gambas). At *El Jardín del Califa (daily | Plaza de España 16 | tel. 9 56 45 17 06 | www.califavejer.com | Moderate)*, Arabian-inspired meals can be enjoyed on a shaded terrace or in the romantic, vaulted dining room. The adjoining hotel *La Casa del Califa (26 rooms | tel. 9 56 44 77 30 | www.lacasadelcalifa.com | Moderate)* offers lovely, bright and atmospheric rooms. For those in the know, Juan Valdés' culinary and grilling expertise is common knowledge. His open-air restaurant INSIDERTIP *La Castillería (closed Fri midday | tel. 9 56 45 14 97 | www.restaurantecastilleria.com | Moderate)* is a verdent oasis in the valley on the other side of the main road in the hamlet Santa Lucía. Information: *Oficina de Turismo (Av. Los Remedios 2 | tel. 9 56 45 17 36 | www.turismovejer.es)*

To the southeast past the natural park is *Barbate* – a little town famous for its fleet of tuna fishing boats and first-class gourmet cooking. The tuna at INSIDERTIP *El Campero (closed Mon | Av. de la Constitución/local 5c | tel. 9 56 43 23 00 | www.restauranteelcampero.es | Moderate–Expensive)* is prepared exceptionally well and makes for a unique experience!

JEREZ DE LA FRONTERA

(150 B3) (*m D6*) **A day in the life in Jerez (pop. 215,000) is best seen on the Calle Larga. Some sit on expensively built terraces with a pint of *fino* (beer); others dress in fine attire and walk up and down the long street.**

Jerez is famous for its wine (or *Sherry*, as foreigners call it). The horse breeders are exceptionally talented and flamenco music still a tradition here. PS fans may see Jerez as the 'Motorcycling Capital of the World' and are familiar with the *Circuito de Jerez* racing circuit. Horse lovers, on the other hand, may know of the city's

---

CITY **WHERE TO START?**
Drivers should head to the centrally located car park located at the **Plaza del Arenal**. A tourist information office is located here where you can get a map of the town. The cathedral, the Alcázar and the city centre are easily to reach here by foot. The Sherry bodegas are on the outskirts of the Old Town and sometimes better reached by car.

famous horse riding school. Either way, Jerez remains a city full of surprises.

Cosy squares, lively bars and tons of contrasts can be found here, a place where the pretty and ugly sides of Andalucía meet. The churches boast exuberant décor and clash with the city's dreary tower blocks. People who feel fortunate to even have a job mingle with those born into rich and influential families.

SIGHTSEEING

ALCÁZAR
This enormous fortress and its massive towers were both built in the 12th century during the Almohad dynasty. The interior boasts Arabian baths, a small mosque and the 18th-century Palacio de Villavicencio, which banned the Moorish flair to the far side of its walls. *Oct–June daily 9.30am–2.30pm, July–Sept Mon–Fri 9.30am–5.30pm, Sat/Sun 9.30am–2.30pm | admission 5 euros, incl. camera obscura 7 euros*

CATHEDRAL
Built in the 18th century, this unique cathedral boasts an imposing flight of steps, a separate bell tower and a mixture of styles including, Gothic, Baroque and neo-Classical elements. *Mon–Sat 10am–6.30pm | admission 5 euros*

CENTRO ANDALUZ DE FLAMENCO
Housed in an 18th-century town palace, this research centre focuses on Spanish flamenco music and is the most important one of its kind. *Mon–Fri 9am–2pm and Wed 4.30pm–7pm | free admission | Plaza San Juan 1 | www.centroandaluzde flamenco.es*

IGLESIA DE SAN DIONISIO
Dedicated to the patron saint of the city and designed in the traditional Mudéjar style, this 15th-century church fronts the Plaza Asunción, one of the most beautiful squares in the city. *Tue–Fri 11am–1pm | admission 1 euro*

REAL ESCUELA ANDALUZA DE ARTE ECUESTRE
The Royal Andalucían School of Equestrian Art holds 18th-century style shows and horse fair galas that last just under two hours. You can choose to visit the Museum for Equestrian Arts and Carriages either with a training presentation or without one *(visita reducida). Times and prices vary, see website for details | Av. Duque de Abrantes | www.realescuela.org*

SHERRY BODEGAS ★ ●
These famous wineries also offer guided tours in English, but it's best to book the tour in advance by calling or going online. Some of the local wineries include the *Bodegas Tradición (Mon–Fri 9am–5pm, July/Aug 8am–3pm, Sat 10am–2pm | 20 euros | Plaza Cordobeses 3 | tel. 9 56 16 86 28 | www.bodegastradicion.es)*, with its significant art collection (e.g. Goya and Velázquez), the *González Byass (for appointments, see website | 15 euros | C/ Manuel María González 12 | tel. 9 56 35 70 16 | www.bodegastiopepe.com)* and the *Lustau (Tours Tue–Fri 10.30am, 12pm, 1pm, 3pm, Mon and Sat 11am and 1pm | from 15 euros | C/ Arcos 53 | tel. 6 74 11 28 12 | www.lustau.es)*

FOOD & DRINK

EL GALLO AZUL
Drink a glass of Sherry, sample the tapas and watch the comings and goings in the pedestrian precinct. No visit to Jerez is complete without a visit to 'The Blue Cockerel'. The restaurant upstairs is more expensive. *Closed Sun | C/ Larga 2 | tel. 9 56 32 61 48 | Budget–Moderate*

INSIDER TIP **EL PASAJE**
This little tapas bar is especially crowded when flamenco is being performed. The atmosphere is warm and rustic, and it's the perfect place to sample some Spanish ham with a glass of Sherry. *Daily | C/ Santa María 8 | tel. 9 56 33 33 59 | Budget*

SHOPPING

Sherry and hand-crafted items in the *Casa del Jerez (C/ Divina Pastora 1 | local 3)*. Excellent Sherry and brandy can be found at *Bodega Rey Fernando de Castilla (Jardinillo 7–11 | www.fernadodecastilla.com)* in the Old Town.

38 euros | C/ Angostillo de Santiago 3 | www.latabernaflamenca.com

WHERE TO STAY

INSIDER TIP **FÉNIX**
Are you looking for a hotel in a quiet side street in the centre? Perhaps a low-priced room that's clean and well-furnished? Then look no further! *16 rooms | C/ Cazón 7 | tel. 9 56 34 52 91 | www.hostal fenix.com | Budget*

HACIENDA DE SAN RAFAEL
Lovely! A 200-year-old manor with pools, a garden and a good restaurant. A wor-

Tap the barrel! A Sherry tasting is initiated at the Jerez winery Bodegas Tradición

ENTERTAINMENT

To start off the night, the bars on the *Plaza del Arenal* and in the *Calle Corredera* are a good starting point.

TABERNA FLAMENCA
Traditional flamenco music performed by a variety of artists. *Tue–Sat, mid-May–Oct, daily 10.30pm | 15 euros, with a meal*

thy 40 km/25 mi trip up north. *Las Cabezas de San Juan | Tel. 9 54 22 71 16 | www. haciendadesanrafael.com | Expensive*

HOTEL PALACIO GARVEY
A former mansion wonderfully located in the city centre, now a four-star hotel with comfortable rooms. Book for cheaper by reserving a room with an online travel company. *16 rooms | C/ Tornería 24 |*

A real classic! The horse races in Sanlúcar de Barrameda

tel. 9 56 32 67 00 | www.hotelpalacio garvey.com | *Moderate*

OFICINA MUNICIPAL DE TURISMO
Plaza del Arenal | tel. 9 56 33 88 74 | www. turismojerez.com

WHERE TO GO

EL PUERTO DE SANTA MARÍA
(150 B4) (*D6*)
Located 14 km/8.7 mi southwest of Jerez at the mouth of the Río Guadalete, this town (pop. 89,000) is a popular destination for Spaniards in the summer. They come for the beaches and exceptional seafood. The slew of restaurants all vie for space around the Ribera del Marisco. The Old Town boasts the 13th-century castle *San Marcos* and the *Iglesia Mayor Prioral* church. *Osborne*, the *bodega* with the bull, *(Guided tours available in English, call to book | 14 euros | tel. 9 56 86 91 00)* is located in the *Calle Moros* 7.

Angel León is one of the biggest chefs in Andalucía. With his more radical culinary creations, he won his restaurant ● *Aponiente (closed Sun, Sept–June closed on Mon, too | C/ Francisco Cossi Ochoa 6 | tel. 9 56 85 18 70 | www.aponiente.com | Expensive)* a Michelin star. A delightful place to stay is in the boutique hotel *Palacio San Bartolomé (11 rooms | C/ San Bartolomé 21 | tel. 9 56 85 09 46 | www. palaciosanbartolome.com | Budget–Moderate)*. Information: *Oficina de Turismo (Plaza del Castillo | tel. 9 9 56 48 37 15 | www.turismoelpuerto.com)*

SANLÚCAR DE BARRAMEDA
(150 A3) (*C6*)
Called 'Olé-Olé' by the locals, Prince Alfonso of Hohenlohe had his luxurious holiday complex built in the city of Sanlúcar (pop. 68,000). He chose the location because it sat oppisite the Doñana National Park, 20 km/12 mi northwest of Jerez at the mouth of the Guadalquivir. For more information, visit the *Centro de Visitantes Fábrica de Hielo (Av. Bajo de*

Guía | tel. 9 56 36 38 13 | www.visitasdo-nana.com), where you can book boat and Jeep trips (daily 10am, April/May and Oct also at 2pm, June–Sept also at 5pm | 35 euros). A number of rustic fish restaurants are located along the river, where horse races are also held every year (mostly in August). One of the most famous places for tapas in Andalucía is the Casa Balbino (Plaza del Cabildo 14 | tel. 9 56 36 05 13 | Budget–Moderate). Be sure to order the tortilla de camarones (EN: crispy prawn fritters) and wash them down with a glass of Manzanilla. To learn how this Sherry is made, visit the Bodegas Barbadillo (daily 10am–3pm | free admission, tasting tours 10 euros | C/ Sevilla 6 | www.barbadillo.com) and its Manzanilla Museum. Not far from there is the ⚬⚬ Castillo de Santiago (Tue–Sat 10am–2.30pm, Sun 11am–2.30pm | 6 euros | Plaza del Castillo), with sweeping views over the city and the river's estuary. The centrally located boutique hotel La Casa Sanlúcar (8 rooms | C/ Ancha 84 | tel. 6 17 57 59 13 | www.lacasasanlucar. com | Budget–Moderate) offers dream-like accommodation. Information: Oficina de Turismo (Calzada de la Duquesa Isabel | Tel. 9 56 36 61 10 | www.sanlucarde barrameda.es)

MÁLAGA

▨▨▨ MAP INSIDE BACK COVER
(152 B–C5) (𝄢 H6) **Málaga is Andalucía's second largest city (pop. 570,000). With its fascinating museums, lively Old Town, enchanting parks and new harbour area, the city is always fun to explore.**

Málaga is no longer just a transfer point for holiday-makers on the Costa del Sol. Ever since the Picasso Museum opened in 2003, the culture in this harbour city has been flourishing. Málaga now offers a variety of new museums, such as the Museo Carmen Thyssen and the Museo Auto-movilístico. An elegant harbour area has even been built for the guests arriving on cruise ships. Apart from the city's old tapas bars, the entire Old Town has been given a new shine. Some of the Malague-ños' beloved rituals include the Easter processions, strolling down the Calle Marqués de Larios, hopping between tapas bars and visiting one of the chiringuitos on Sunday. At these beach bars, sardines are grilled on wooden skewers over an open fire. In short, Málaga is a city you'll quickly fall in love with!

SIGHTSEEING

ALCAZABA ⚬⚬
At one point in time, this 11th-century Moorish fortification was supposedly even more beautiful than the Alhambra in Granada. Called the Alcazaba (from the Arabic al-qasbah, meaning 'citadel'), it now boasts tranquil gardens with relaxing water features and romantic corners with beautiful views. Daily 9am–6pm, April–Oct til 8pm | admission 2.20 euros, Alcazaba and Gibralfaro 3.55 euros

> 🏙 **WHERE TO START?**
> To get a general feel for your surroundings, start by getting a view of the city and sea from the top of Gibralfaro. A fortress stands at the top of this hill, and a beautiful trail will lead you to the top. Below in the city, a good starting point is the **Plaza de la Marina**, where there's a car park and information centre. From here, you can reach all the attractions on foot.

CASTILLO DE GIBRALFARO ⊰⊱

Málaga's second Moorish fortress towers over the city from its hilltop site. It's linked to the Alcazaba by a walled-in footpath that leads up the hill. It's worth visiting the Gibralfaro just to get a view over Málaga and its harbour. *Daily 9am–6pm, April–Oct til 8pm | admission 2.20 euros, Gibralfaro and Alcazaba 3.55 euros, free on Sun after 2pm*

CATHEDRAL DE LA ENCARNACIÓN

The Malagueños call their cathedral *La Manquita*, 'the one-armed lady'. Its construction dragged on for more than 250 years (1528–1783). With the locals no longer wanting to pay a special tax to finance all the pomp, its second tower was never completed. Especially noteworthy are the 17th-century choir stalls carved by Pedro de Mena and the 4000-pipe organ. *Mon–Fri 10am–6pm, Sat 10am–5pm | admission 5 euros*

MUELLE UNO

Málaga's modern harbour is decked out in white. From its promenade, you can casually walk towards the lighthouse. In the evening, there are plenty of bars where you can enjoy a drink. You can also view some exciting art at the Parisian ★ *Centre Pompidou (daily 9.30am–8pm | admission 7 euros | centrepompidou-malaga.eu)*. Here, in the Spanish branch, you find changing exhibitions for contemporary art.

MUSEO CARMEN THYSSEN

It took four years to construct the Palacio Villalón in the Old Town of Málaga. This cultural highlight cost 25 million euros and is now home to 230 works of art. This famous, first-class collection belongs to the Baroness Carmen Thyssen-Bornemisza. Among the works are 19th-century paintings with mostly Andalucían motifs. The artists include Joaquín Sorolla, Mariano Fortuny and Julio Romero de Torres. *Tue–Sun 10am–8pm | admission 6 euros | C/ Compañía 10 | www.carmen thyssenmalaga.org*

MUSEO PICASSO MÁLAGA ★

The Picasso Museum in Málaga is a must for all Picasso fans – and for those who have not yet formed an opinion about

Málaga's new harbour promenade: a modern design or a clean area for cruise passengers?

the artist. Picasso's daughter-in-law and her son, Bernard, have given the museum more than 200 works – or lent them as permanent loans – covering all of the artist's creative periods. The collection is housed in the beautifully restored Palacio de Buenavista. *Mar–June and Sept/Oct daily 10am–7pm, July/Aug 10am–8pm, Nov–Feb 10am–6pm | admission 7 euros | C/ de San Agustín 8 | www.museopicassomalaga.org*

TABACALERA ●

He checks out the cars while she observes the art? Not really the best plan. Why not look at them both together? Located in the old tobacco factory south of the centre, the *Museo Automovilístico y de la Moda (Tue–Sun 10am–7pm | admission 8.50 euros | www.museoautomovilmalaga.com)* and the *Colección del Museo Ruso (Tue–Sun 9.30am–8pm | 8 euros | www.coleccionmuseoruso.es)* has some truly impressive exhibitions. 'Cars are art' is the message proclaimed at the car museum, where roughly 100 beautifully designed automobiles, stemming from all decades, are placed in halls alongside 200 haute couture clothing articles by Chanel, Dior and many others. At the Russian National Museum, Museo Ruso, a portion of their giant art collection is on display. You may know the works by the Russian artist Marc Chagall, a Constructivist from the 1920s. The giant paintings stemming from the 19th centruy are truly impressive. *Av. Sor Teresa Prat 15*

Gender mainstreaming is addressed at the Tabacalera: cars and fashion

FOOD & DRINK

Chiringuitos is the name given to the popular beach bars and restaurants in Andalucía. In Málaga, they're a culinary staple. In summer, the fish is grilled over an open flame. You can taste it, e.g. on the beaches of Malagueta and Pedregalejo.

ANTIGUA CASA DE GUARDIA

The most unspoilt *bodega* in Málaga – since 1840! Good wine and fresh seafood. *Closed Sunday evening | Alameda Principal 18 | tel. 9 52 21 46 80 | antiguacasadeguardia.com | Budget*

JOSÉ CARLOS GARCÍA ●

Top chef José Carlos García operates in a super-deluxe restaurant in the new harbour area. His classic *Café de Paris* at *C/ Vélez-Malaga 8* is still running, too. Gourmet menus from 66 euros. *Closed Sun/Mon | Plaza de la Capilla/Muelle Uno | tel. 9 52 00 35 88 | www.restaurantejcg.com | Expensive*

INSIDER TIP▶ LA RECOVA

Some like to go into the little shops to see what Spanish handicrafts they may find: ceramics, leather articles, wines, used goods – the list is endless. Others get a shot at a table to sample the country-style tortillas, Manchego cheese, or blood sausage (SP: *morcilla*). Some do both! Have a snack and then check out the most unusual souvenirs on offer! *Closed Sun | Pasaje Nuestra Señora de los Dolores de San Juan 5 | tel. 9 52 21 67 94 | www.larecova.es | Budget*

EL PIMPI

Legendary tapas restaurant near the Picasso Museum. *Closed Mon afternoon | C/ Granada 62 | tel. 9 52 22 89 90 | Moderate*

ENTERTAINMENT

Málaga's turbulent nightlife takes place around the *Plaza de la Merced*, in the *Calle Granada* and at the new harbour. In summer, the city's night owls also flock to the beaches and into the beach bars around the Pedregalejo district.

WHERE TO STAY

INSIDER TIP **HOTEL DEL PINTOR**

Centrally located in the Old Town, this unique boutique hotel was decorated by painter Pepe Bornoy from Málaga. Red and white creatively complement the chic interior design. Furnished rooms with a modern look, all at a good price. *17 rooms | C/ Álamos 27 | tel. 9 52 06 09 80 | hoteldelpintor.com | Budget–Moderate*

ROOM MATE VALERIA

Modern living and design. This upscale hotel seems to be the ideal place for urban nomads (with a proper income). Everything is good and comfortable here: the location, the view, WiFi connection, rooftop bar and pool; and its fitness room. *61 rooms | Plaza Poeta Alfonso Canales 5 | tel. 9 52 06 04 01 | www.room-matehotels.com | Moderate–Expensive*

Impressive megalithic graves in Antequera: the Dólmenes de Menga y Viera

INFORMATION

OFICINA MUNICIPAL DE TURISMO
Plaza de la Marina 11 (branch offices Plaza de la Aduana and Av. de Cervantes 1) | tel. 9 51 92 60 20 | www.malagaturismo.com

OFICINA DE TURISMO DE LA JUNTA DE ANDALUCÍA
Plaza de la Constitución 7 | tel. 9 51 30 89 11

WHERE TO GO

ANTEQUERA (152 B4) (*☍ H5*)

There are two megalithic burial chambers 50 km/31 mi north of Málaga near Antequera (pop. 41,000): the *Dólmenes de Menga y Viera* (2500 BC) and the *Dolmen del Romeral (every Tue–Sun 9am–3pm, mid-Sept–mid-June till 5pm | free admission)* (1800 BC). Made of stones weighing several tonnes, both chambers have been well preserved. A walk around the Old Town of Antequera is also worthwhile, with its beautiful Baroque churches and ⚙ *Castillo Árabe*. The restaurant on the Plaza de Santa María *El Escribano (closed Tue | tel. 9 52 70 65 33 | Budget–Moderate)* offers a sun terrace and regional specialities. Information: *Oficina Municipal de Turismo (Plaza de San Sebastián 7 | tel. 9 52 70 25 05 | turismo.antequera.es)*

EL TORCAL ★ (152 B5) (*☍ H6*)

15 km/9 mi south of Antequera is a fantastic, erosion-induced rocky landscape. The *Paraje Natural El Torcal* boasts karst formations you'll want to explore. The hiking trails start at the information centre's car park. Africa can be seen from the ⚙ *Mirador las Ventanillas* on a clear day. On the south side of the hill is the wolf sanctuary *Lobo Park Antequera (see p. 127),* where you can watch these wild animals.

GARGANTA DEL CHORRO ★ (152 A4) (*☍ G6*)

Afraid of heights? Than don't read any further! This beautiful gorge lies 60 km/37 mi northwest of Málaga. It reaches distances up to 400 m/1312 ft high and 10 m/33 ft wide. Up until a few years ago, the old *Caminito del Rey (admission 10 euros | www.caminitodelrey.info)* was the 'King's Pathway' for adrenaline junkies. Bored with life, they dreamt of crossing the gorge to feel the rush of walking across the 'world's most dangerous trail'. After some fatal accidents, the government sealed off the trail and installed a new wooden walkway. Having reopened in 2015, the trail now sits approximately 100 m/328 ft above the old one, but there aren't any crumbling parts to cross over anymore. Its 7.7 km/4.8 mi length, and 3 km/1.9 mi height have been turned into a vie ferrata, but make a reservation soon if you'd like to cross it!

MIJAS (152 B6) (*☍ G7*)

The city of Mijas (pop. 78,000) is 35 km/22 mi southwest of Málaga. Its beautiful centre attracts many day visitors, but it's best to stay over at the *Hotel TRH Mijas (204 rooms | C/ Tamisa 2 | tel. 9 52 48 58 00 | www.trhhoteles.com | Moderate)*. Wake up early and walk to the 16th-century pilgrimage church the ⚙ *Santuario de la Virgen de la Peña*. Information: *Oficina de Turismo (Plaza Virgen de la Peña 2a | tel. 9 52 58 90 34 | turismo.mijas.es)*

TORREMOLINOS (152 B6) (*☍ H6–7*)

It's hard to imagine that this resort town was once a modest village in the 1960s. 13 km/8 mi west of Málaga, it's filled with hotels and apartment blocks and at least 300 bars, restaurants and discos, all densely packed along the 7 km/4.3 mi-long beach. With there not being any sites of interest here, visitors come for fun under the sun, entertainment and the beach. Torremolinos (pop. 68,000) is built around the holiday-makers, accounting for one third of all the hotel accommodation on the Costa del Sol.

If you're overwhelmed by the number of restaurants here, head over to the *La Carihuela* province, an old fishing district where you can still get *pescaítos fritos* (EN: fried fish). If you're looking for a nice hotel, *La Luna Blanca (7 rooms | Pasaje Cerrillo 2 | tel. 9 52 05 37 11 | www. hotellalunablanca.com | Moderate)* is peacefully located 300 m/984 ft from La Carihuela beach. Information: *Oficina de Turismo (Plaza de la Independencia 1 | tel. 9 52 37 42 31 | www.torremolinos.es)*

MARBELLA

(153 A6) *(ᗰ G7)* **It's not yet all that long ago when Marbella (pop. 140,000) was seen as Spain's hotspot for jet setters – that is, until Mallorca outstripped it.**

Although the city isn't as popular as it used to be, it still upholds a sophisticated reputation. There's a beautiful sandy beach located in front of the rows of hotels and apartment blocks, and its old, whitewashed village is landscaped with

> **CITY WHERE TO START?**
> The **Plaza de los Naranjos** in the Old Town and the seaside promenade are well worth seeing. The multi-storey car park next to the Park La Alameda lies right between the two. Bus lines 1, 2, 3, 6 and 7 go to the city centre. To reach the luxury marina Puerto Banús, take bus line 1 from 'Marbella Centro'.

many flowers. There are also plenty of upscale restaurants, shops and clubs in *Puerto Banús,* a marina 6 km/3.7 mi further west. You can get there by boat or by walking 90-minutes across the seaside promenade.

SIGHTSEEING

CASCO ANTIGUO (OLD TOWN)

This Old Town's beauty takes everyone by surprise. Stroll through its charming alleyways. Landscaped by flowers, they lead to the *Plaza de los Naranjos* (EN: Plaza of Orange Trees), which boasts an octagonal marmor fountain, a 16th-century courthouse and a small church that's almost just as old.

FOOD & DRINK

INSIDER TIP BAR ALTAMIRANO

A loud and lively sports bar. The walls are covered with the fan scarves of many European football teams. But the best part about this place is the tasty fish and seafood served here! *Daily | Plaza Altamirano 3 | tel. 9 52 82 49 32 | www.baraltamirano.es | Budget*

INSIDER TIP EL GALLO

Even in rich Marbella, it's possible to find an affordable restaurant serving simple Andalucían food. Situated in the Old Town, the restaurant belongs to a hostel that's equally noteworthy. *Closed Thu | C/ Lobatas 46 | tel. 9 52 82 79 98 | Budget*

ENTERTAINMENT

There is an incredible number of bars, pubs and discos with a tendency more towards the sophisticated. The younger crowd meets up in the Old Town around Peral and Mesoncillo streets, on the Plaza de los Olivos or in the Calle Pantaleón. One of the most popular places in the Old Town is *Town House* in the Calle Álamo.

Those who prefer things a little quieter should head for the bars in the Calle Camilo José Cela. The nightlife for the rich and beautiful takes place in Puerto Banús. Check things out in the *Guía Magazine Dia y Noche* (at the tourist information centre) or under *www.guiamarbella.com*

WHERE TO STAY

FUERTE MARBELLA

This hotel has kept its great location for over 50 years. Close to the Old Town, it sits directly on the beach promenade and beach. Great breakfast, friendly staff and a beautiful garden. *263 rooms | Av. El Fuerte | tel. 9 52 86 15 00 | www.fuerte hoteles.com | Expensive*

MARBELLA CLUB

This is hands down the most famous hotel in the city. Built to be a luxurious bungalow complex, it saw the beginning of Marbella's jet-set era in the 1960s. *121 rooms, 14 villas | Bulevar Príncipe Alfonso de Hohenlohe | tel. 9 52 82 22 11 | www.marbellaclub.com | Expensive*

INSIDER TIP **LA MORADA MÁS HERMOSA**

A charming, tiny hotel with individually furnished rooms. The room in the tower and Room 2 with a roof terrace and lemon tree are particularly lovely. *7 rooms | C/ Montenebros 16a | tel. 9 52 92 44 67 | www. lamoradamashermosa.com | Moderate*

INFORMATION

OFICINA DE TURISMO

Plaza de los Naranjos 1 | tel. 9 52 76 87 07 | www.turismo.marbella.es).

The beach in Marbella: the sea ahead and the lovely Old Town behind

A fantasy world: Cueva de Nerja

NERJA

(153 D5) (𝄞 J6) A beautiful town (pop. 21,000) on the eastern side of the Costa del Sol. Although small, the beaches are still jam-packed in summer.

In *Nerja*'s centre, the ⚡ *Balcón de Europa* sits above the sea on a rocky promontory. It offers sweeping views over the water from its wide viewing terrace. Before becoming a tourist destination, Nerja was once a fishing village. The romantic, little bays below symbolise this past. Wider beaches are located on both sides of the centre. Despite all the hustle and bustle here, a pleasant village-like atmosphere can still be felt.

SIGHTSEEING

CUEVA DE NERJA

Despite the music and wide, paved paths, the stalactites and stalagmites are still incredible to see in this 4 km/2.5 mi-long cave. A great music festival happens every year here in July. *Daily 9am–4pm, July/Aug until 6.30pm | admission 10 euros | www.cuevadenerja.es*

FOOD & DRINK

JULIES & VALERI'S

A great atmosphere with delicious tapas, many being vegetarian. The restaurant's English-Cuban hosts welcome you from the moment you walk in the door. *Daily | Plaza Balcón de Europa | tel. 6 33 72 83 16 | Budget–Moderate*

MO GASTROTAPAS

This restaurant is located a bit outside of the centre, but it's still well worth the trip! Delicious tapas creations, like fresh tuna fish with vanilla carrots and avocados. *Daily | C/ Andalucía 27 | tel. 9 52 52 00 32 | www.mogastrotapas.es | Moderate*

WHERE TO STAY

MAR AZUL ⚡

A cosy *hostal* near the Playa de la Torrecilla. Most rooms have a view of the sea. *10 rooms | Av. Mediterráneo 12 | tel. 9 52 52 41 91 | Budget–Moderate*

INSIDER TIP ▶ PARAÍSO DEL MAR ⚡

Top location, perfect view. Perched above the seaside, it offers views over an endless sea. A homey-feeling hotel with cosy corners, terraces, a pool and luxurious rooms that are all lovely furnished. *18 rooms | Prolongación de Carabeo 22 | tel. 9 52 52 16 21 | www.hotel paraisodelmar.es | Moderate–Expensive*

OFICINA DE TURISMO
C/ Carmen 1 | tel. 9 52 52 15 31 | www.
nerja.org

WHERE TO GO

FRIGILIANA (153 D5) *(∅ J6)*
Escape the Costa del Sol for a day by going just a few miles north of Nerja. In this whitewashed village (pop. 3000), you'll walk through narrow streets and get a feeling of what life was like during the Moorish era. Ceramics and sugar cane molasses are old in the *Ingenio*, the largest building at the foot of the Barrio Mudéjar. The *Fábrica de Miel de Caña* has a unique taste and is rare to find in Europe.

Enjoy a meal with a view at ↙ *El Jardín (closed Mon | C/ Santo Cristo| tel. 9 52 53 31 85 | Moderate)*. The country hotel *Posada Morisca (12 rooms | C/ Loma de la Cruz | Tel. 9 52 53 41 51 | www.laposadamorisca.com | Moderate)* is just outside of town and offers a view over the region's landscape. Frigiliana is another great place if you'd like to see more whitewashed villages in the Axarquía and other natural parks, e.g. the *Sierras de Tejeda* and *Almijara y Alhama*. Information: *Oficina de Turismo (Cuesta del Apero | tel. 9 52 53 42 61 | www.turismo-frigiliana.es)*

INSIDER TIP MARO (153 D5) *(∅ J6)*
Located 4 km/2.5 mi east of Nerja, this whitewashed village is still an insider tip, possibly because it takes walking a bit to reach the local beach. With tourism being so scarce here, the village has kept its quiet and genuine feel. In the centre, there's a ↙ viewing deck next to the church *Virgen de las Maravillas*. The hotel *Casa Maro (9 rooms | C/ Maravillas |*

tel. 6 27 95 84 56 | Budget–Moderate) offers beautiful Mediterranean-style apartments with a view of the sea.

RONDA

(151 E3) *(∅ F6)* **Romantic ⭐ Ronda (pop. 35,000) is perched on a rocky plateau with a vertical drop of 165 m/541 ft. The town is divided by a deep ravine (Spanish: *tajo*).**
The ↙ *Puente Nuevo*, a spectacular masterpiece of 18th-century engineering, links the old part of Ronda (called *La Ciudad*) with its newer part *(El Mercadillo)*. The newer part is north of the *tajo* and from the 16th century. There are still traces of the Romans and especially the Moors who were first defeated by the Catholic monarchy in 1485. Present-day 'romantic' Ronda, however, is a town of the 18th-century *Casa Maro*. It's been praised by writers like Ernest Hemmingway, who used the town as a setting for his novel *For Whom the Bell Tolls*.

LOW BUDGET

When in Cádiz, keep a lookout for a *freiduría*, where you can buy cheap fried fish.

Want to visit a world heritage site for free? Our ancestors built the *Dolmen de Menga* and *de Viera* 4000 years ago in Antequera.

● Explore Málaga with a free audio guide. MP3 players can also be rented at the tourist information centre on the Plaza de la Marina.

RONDA

SIGHTSEEING

BAÑOS ÁRABES

Going downhill is easy, but what about the way back up? It's best not to think about it and just enjoy the beauty of these well-maintained Arab baths. Nowhere in Andalucía will you find a columned hall this well-preserved. If we've piqued your interest and you'd like to take an Arab bath yourself, we recommend the *Hammam Aguas de Ronda (Mon–Fri 10am–6pm, in summer till 7pm, Sat/Sun 10am–3pm | C/ San Miguel 12 | www.hammamaguasderonda.com | admission 3.50 euros)*. It's just a few metres away.

IGLESIA SANTA MARÍA LA MAYOR

Ronda's main church is on the most beautiful square in town, the *Plaza de la Duquesa de Parcent*, landscaped with shady palms and bay trees. Inside the entrance a richly decorated prayer niche that once formed part of the mosque that stood on this site, leads off to one side. In the church, built after the Christian conquest of Ronda, Gothic and Renaissance elements clash like water and oil with one another. *Daily 10am–6pm, June–Sept till 8pm | admission 4.50 euros*

LA MINA DE AGUA

The 18th-centruy town palace *Casa del Rey Moro (daily 10am–6.30pm, April–Oct till 8pm | admission 5 euros)* on the edge of the *tajo* is rather run-down, but still intriguing. A Moorish king had a complicated arrangement of steps hewn inside the rock in the 14th century which lead 60 m/197 ft down into the depths below. The *Mina de Agua* (lit: 'water mine')

Spectacular engineering! The Puente Nuevo connects the divide in Ronda

served as both a fountain and a defence system. The palace also has a nice and peaceful garden café with a view of the gorge. It's located below the garden and free of charge to enter.

PALACIO DE MONDRAGÓN

One of Ronda's beautiful town palaces with inner courtyards in the Mudéjar style. It is now the *Museo Municipal (Mon–Fri 10am–7pm, in winter 6pm, Sat/ Sun 10am–3pm | admission 3 euros)* with replicas of Stone Age burial chambers and caves.

PLAZA DE TOROS

The bullring from 1785 is the oldest in Spain and the only one where the two-tiered rows of seats, surrounding an unusually large arena, are completely roofed over. The adjoining *Museo Tauri-*

no *(daily 10am–6pm, April–Sept till 8pm | admission 7 euros | www.rmcr.org)*, provides a good introduction to the history of bullfighting.

PUERTA DE ALMOCÁBAR

The gate with pointed horseshoe arches at the southern end of the Ciudad is a remnant of Moorish fortifications. Next to it is a church that the Catholic monarchs Ferdinand and Isabella had built. Called the *Espíritu Santo* and built on the foundations of a Moorish castle, its design is simple yet particularly beautiful. *Mon– Sat 10am–2pm | admission 1 euro*

FOOD & DRINK

CASA MATEOS

Great wine and tapas – not your typical run of the mill. This small bar is so nice that you'll most likely want to stay longer than you initially intended. *Closed Sun evening and Mon | C/ Jerez 6 | tel. 6 70 67 97 62 | Moderate*

INSIDER TIP EL LECHUGUITA

Simply delicious! A bar without the chi-chi. Mouth-watering tapas and appetisers. Orders are made by simply marking off what you'd like on a slip of paper; perfect for those struggling to speak Spanish. *Closed Sun | C/ Virgen de los Remedios 35 | tel. 9 52 87 80 76 | Budget*

PEDRO ROMERO

There's sure to be restaurants with better ratings, but to see the walls' bullfighting memorabilia makes the experience worthwhile. The atmosphere is rustic yet charming. The smell and taste of the cuisine stands out because they aren't following any recent culinary trends. Their *rabo de toro* (EN: oxtail) is especially delicious. *Daily | C/ Virgen de la Paz 18 | tel. 9 52 87 11 10 | Moderate–Expensive*

WHERE TO STAY

ALAVERA DE LOS BAÑOS
Below the Old Town near the Arabian baths, this tastefully decorated hotel is the ideal place to relax in, thanks to its peaceful location, garden, pool and tasty breakfast. *9 rooms | C/ San Miguel | tel. 9 52 87 91 43 | www.alaveradelos banos.com | Moderate*

CATALONIA REINA VICTORIA ☆
This exquisite hotel offers lovely views and a garden. Today, its interior has been completely revamped and is now a modern boutique hotel and spa. *95 rooms | C/ Jerez 25 | tel. 9 52 87 12 40 | www.hoteles-catalonia.com | Moderate–Expensive*

MONTELIRIO
Located in the Old Town in a historical building on the edge of the gorge, this hotel has charmingly designed its rooms to reflect the style of the past century. *15 rooms | C/ Tenorio 8 | tel. 9 52 87 38 55 | www.hotelmontelirio.com | Expensive*

RONDA
This tiny family-run hotel is slightly above the Casa del Rey Moro. Breakfast is served in the tastefully modern rooms. *5 rooms | Rueda Doña Elvira 12 | tel. 9 52 87 22 32 | www.hotelronda.net | Budget–Moderate*

INFORMATION

OFICINA DE TURISMO
Paseo de Blas Infante | tel. 9 52 18 71 19 | www.turismoderonda.es

WHERE TO GO

CUEVA DE LA PILETA
(151 D–E3) (*M F6*)
27 km/17 mi southwest of Ronda, these prehistoric caves boast rock drawings 27,000 years old. *1-hour guided tours in summer: Mon–Fri 10.30am, 1pm, 4pm and 6pm, Sat/Sun 10am/11am/12pm/1pm/4pm/5pm, in winter Mon–Fri 11.30am/1pm/5pm, Sat/Sun 11am/12pm/1pm/4pm/5pm | admission 8 euros*

TARIFA

(151 D6) (*M E8*) **The atmosphere in ★ Tarifa (pop. 18,000) feels a bit like Goa or Australia but with a big dollop of Moorish history thrown in for good measure.**
Here at the most southern tip of Spain, the wind blows through the straits. Although this may make going to the beach unpleasant for sunbathers, surfers and kite flyers seem to not get enough of it. Many travel to Tarifa, in fact, specifically because it's a 'high wind area'. Located on the harbour, the Moorish castle *Castillo de Guzmán el Bueno (Easter–Oct daily 9.30am–8.30pm, Nov–Easter Tue–Sun 11.30am–5.30pm | admission 4 euros)* dates back to the 10th century and has been kept well-preserved over the years.

FOOD & DRINK

CHILIMOSA ☻
Only vegetarian cuisine is served at this charming little restaurant. Some dishes are prepared with organically produced ingredients, and all meals (e.g. the curries or wheat gluten kabab) can also be ordered to go. *Daily | C/ Peso 6 | tel. 9 56 68 50 92 | Budget*

MORILLA
Always packed with guests, this bar restaurant on the Plaza Oviedo seems to be the town's living room. Simple and traditional cooking. *Daily | C/ Sancho IV El Bravo 2 | tel. 9 56 68 17 57 | Budget*

SPORTS & ACTIVITIES

Wind surfing, kite surfing, wave surfing, stand-up paddling, horseback riding, mountain biking, climbing, paragliding – no matter what you're looking for, everything is possible here. For more information, go to the tourist information centre. One- or two-day trips to neighbouring Tangier in Morocco are on offer at the harbour: *FRS (operates crossings several times a day | day-trip 59 euros | tel. 9 56 68 18 30 | www.frs.es)*. Boat trips with whalewatching: *Firmm (30 euros | tel. 9 56 62 70 08 | www.firmm.org)*

WHERE TO STAY

DOS MARES

The nicest hotel on the *Los Lances* surfing beach, in the Andalucían style, with a first-class restaurant. *48 rooms | N 340, km 79.5 | tel. 9 56 68 40 35 | www.dosmareshotel.com | Moderate–Expensive*

INSIDER TIP ▸ MISIANA

This classy hotel was once a simple yet modern city residence and home to the Spanish pop-singer Ana Torroja. Today, it has been relaunched and remodelled with a warm, white interior design. Known for its amazing breakfast, *Hotel Misiana* remains a popular place to stay for many guests. *15 rooms | C/ Sánchez IV | tel. 9 56 62 70 83 | www.misiana.com | Budget–Moderate*

POSADA LA SACRISTÍA

In Tarifa, there are a lot of guests looking for smaller hotels with an exquisite design. The Sacristía is one of the most beautiful you'll find. Their rooms are individually designed with a special flair of their own. They offer a small sun terrace, a lounge restaurant and relaxing massages to make you feel completely spoilt. *10 rooms | C/ San Donato 8 | tel. 9 56 68 17 59 | www.lasacristia.net | Moderate–Expensive*

Kites and a view of Africa: Europe ends in Tarifa

TARIFA

OFICINA DE TURISMO
Paseo de la Alameda | tel. 9 56 68 09 93 | tarifaturismo.com

WHERE TO GO

INSIDER TIP ▶ BOLONIA ●
(150 C6) (*ℳ E8*)

About 25 km/14 mi northwest of Tarifa, you'll find a sweeping bay with a fine sandy beach (by far the most beautiful one around!) as well as a few *hostales* and *chiringuitos*. *Los Jerezanos (25 rooms | C/ Lentiscal 5 | tel. 9 56 68 85 92 | Budget–Moderate)* is a family-run hotel and restaurant right on the beach. Next to it are the ruins of the small Roman settlement *Baelo Claudia* with a circular route for visitors *(mid-June–mid-Sept Tue–Sat 9am–3pm, mid-Sept–March 9am–6pm, April–mid-June 9am–8pm, every Sun 9am–3pm | free admission for EU citizens).*

INSIDER TIP ▶ CASTELLAR DE LA FRONTERA (151 D5) (*ℳ E7*)

A magical place located 50 km/31 mi northeast of Tarifa. Built on the top of a hill, 70 houses jostle for space within the walls of this Moorish fortress dating back to the 13th and 14th centuries. Cars stay parked outside of the castle gate. You only need a few minutes to explore the few cobbled lanes full of climbing plants and to take in the view from the ⬈ *mirador* that overlooks the reservoir below. In 1971 the former residents of the *castillo* moved out and built a new village down on the plain. Escapists then moved into the empty houses. A cosy restaurant *(daily)* and your own little cottage can now be found in *Castillo de Castellar (9 houses sleeping 2–6 | C/ Rosario 3 | tel. 9 56 69 31 50 | www.tugasa.com | Moderate)*.

GIBRALTAR (151 D5–6) (*ℳ F8*)

Crossing the border from Andalucía, you enter another world. Befittingly, you must have your passport with you. Be prepared for extensive and meticulous searches. 40 km/25 mi northeast of Tarifa is Gibraltar (pop. 29,000), a very English area. The Rock of Gibralter has been a British Overseas Territory since 1713. Some 7 million visitors come here every year to explore the massive Rock that is home to the famous apes and to shop in the *Main Street* with its duty-free shopping (they do accept euros). It is well worth visiting the ⬈ *Upper Rock Nature Reserve.* Here you'll find the limestone caves of *St Michael's Cave*, the *Great Siege Tunnels* (a defence system from the end of the 18th century) and the *Apes' Den* (where the famous Barbary macaques leap around), which offers a beautiful view. The reserve is best reached by cable car *(daily 9.30am–5.15pm, April–Oct till 7.15pm | roundtrip 14 pounds, incl. the nature reserve 22 pounds). Dolphin watching (approx. 30 euros/person)* is also very popular. There are several companies operating, mostly out of Marina Bay. For fish and chips, steak or a good cup of coffee, *Jury's Café & Wine Bar (daily | 275 Main Street | tel. 00350 20 06 78 98 |www.jurysgibraltar.com | Moderate)* is a nice place if you're looking for good British atmosphere. For a stylish night in Gibraltar, the *Bristol Hotel* is a good location *(60 rooms | 8–10 Cathedral Square | tel. 00350 20 07 68 00 | www.bristolhotel.gi | Moderate)*. Their historical, colonial-style building is centrally located. If you intend to stay until the evening, drive to Gibraltar by car. The wait at customs on the way back is not usually very long. Or else park just before the border on the Spanish side in *La Línea*. From there, Main Street is a 15 min. walk, or hop in a taxi after crossing the border. Customs regulations are those of a non-EU country – goods to the value of 300 euros, 200 cigarettes and 1 litre of spirits are duty-free. Information: *Gibraltar Tourist Board (Cathedral Square | tel. 00350 20 07 49 50 | www.visitgibraltar.gi)*

THE WHITE TOWNS

From a distance, it looks like people from all walks of life came to this green, brown and grey landscape in Andalucía to paint sections of it in shimmering white. ⭐ **The White Towns are more or less perfectly whitewashed buildings. The colour reflects the sun and prevents the interior from turning into an oven.** Thanks to an especially clever idea to promote tourism, the white villages and little towns between Ronda and Arcos de la Frontera have virtually become a brand name.

SIGHTSEEING

ARCOS DE LA FRONTERA
(150 C3) (*𝄞 E6*)
The heart of this town (pop. 31,000) beats at the Plaza del Cabildo. The first place you'll want to go is atop the 🔅 *Mirador de la Peña Nueva*. The view over the cliff is simply breathtaking. Arcos is like a white slab on an ochre-coloured rocky cliff that, to the southwest, drops vertically 160 m/525 ft to the Río Guadalete below. Opposite the Mirador is the 15th-century basilica *Santa María* with its huge bell tower. To the left, you'll see the *town hall* with its beautiful *artesonado* ceiling. Behind it, there's a Moorish castle that's more than 1000 years old. On the right-hand side is the *Parador (24 rooms |*

tel. 9 56 70 05 00 | Moderate–Expensive). The rooms' balconies look straight down to the bottom of the cliff.

The *C/ de los Escribanos*, with its stone arches, leads down the side of the Parador to the labyrinthine streets of the Old Town. After a short distance, you'll reach the *Convento de Mercedarias Descalzas (Plazuela de Botica 2). (1642, Baroque retable, daily 8.30am–2.30pm, 5pm–7pm | Plazuela de Botica 2)*. Here INSIDER TIP the nuns sells little homemade cakes through a hatch. Accommodation is

Spanish or British? For some residents it's an irrelevant question in Gibraltar

available at the *Casa Grande (7 rooms | C/ Maldonado 10 | tel. 9 56 70 39 30 | www.lacasagrande.net | Budget–Moderate)*. This townhouse full of character is right on the cliff edge. The patio and the beautifully furnished library are a delight. In the historical Upper Town, there are plenty of simple bars and restaurants you can enjoy. Even the locals love going to *Bar La Cárcel (daily | C/ Deán Espinosa 18 | tel. 9 56 70 04 10 | Budget)*. Right next to it is the bar *Tablao de Manuela*, where flamenco artists perform on a regular basis. Those who prefer things a little more stylish will find what they are looking for in the restaurant *El Corregidor (daily | Plaza del Cabildo | tel. 9 56 70 05 00 | Expensive)* in the Parador Hotel. Information: *Oficina Municipal de Turismo (Cuesta de Belén 5 | tel. 9 56 70 22 64 | turismoarcos. com)*

INSIDER TIP ▶ **BENADALID**
(151 E4) (*ळ F6–7*)
The Moorish fortress still dominates the area up above the valley, but its walls now enclose a cemetery of white sepulchral niches. Benadalid is an enchanting spot on the Serranía de Ronda. On the main road, you'll find the only *hostal* in the village – simple but well maintained – *Aguayar (5 rooms | A369 at km 25 | tel. 9 52 15 27 68 | Budget)*.

CASARES (151 E4) (*ळ F7*)
55 km/34 mi west of Marbella is the whitewashed town of Casares – picturesquely situated in the Sierra Bermeja and crowned with a Moorish ♨ *Castillo*. Many restaurants are on the Plaza España. One of the best hotels in Andalucía is the golf hotel *Finca Cortesin (67 suites | Ctra. de Casares | tel. 9 52 93 78 00 | www.fincacortesin.com | Expensive)*. The grounds are exquisite, the restaurant is outstanding and plenty of sport activities are offered. Along the coast on the MA-8300 at km 7 is the rustic restaurant *Venta García (closed Mon | tel. 9 52 89 41 91 | Moderate)*, serving crispy, grilled lamb chops. Information: *Oficina de Turismo (C/ Carrera 51 | tel. 9 52 89 55 21 | www.casares.es)*

GAUCÍN (151 D4) (*ळ F7*)
The British love this pretty white town in the Serranía de Ronda. Many artists live here and present their work in the town's galleries and studios. This is a lovely place to spend a few days in. Book a room at the *La Fructuosa (5 rooms | C/ Convento 67 | tel. 6 17 69 27 84 | www.lafructuosa.com | Moderate)*, where the food is an experience in itself *(closed Mon/Tue | Moderate)*. The late 9th-century ♨ *Castillo de Águila (daily 10am–1.30pm, 4pm–7.30pm)* offers a great view over the village. Information: *Oficina del Turismo (Paseo Ana Toval | tel. 9 52 15 10 00 | www.gaucin.es)*

GRAZALEMA (151 D3) (*ळ F6*)
This little whitewashed town (pop. 2200) is at the foot of the *Peñón Grande* (EN: Large Rock) and in the centre of the *Sierra de Grazalema Natural Park*. The *Plaza de España* is perfect for tourist shopping (beautiful, hand-woven blankets!), drinking and dining. Located in the middle of hot Andalucía, this is where Spain gets most of its rainfall. Appearing like Christmas trees, the Spanish firs especially enjoy the rain and grow everywhere. Just outside of town is an excellent and affordable 4-star hotel: the ♨ *Fuerte Grazalema (77 rooms | Baldío de los Alamillos | A-372 at km 53 | tel. 9 56 13 30 00 | www.fuerte.com | Moderate)*, with a pool and wonderful view of the mountains. A less expensive hotel is the lovely *Casa de las Piedras (30 rooms | C/ Las Piedras 32 | tel. 9 56 13 20 14 | www.casadelaspiedras.org | Budget)*. Information: *Oficina de Turismo (Plaza Asomaderos 3 | tel. 9 56 13 20 52)*

SETENIL DE LAS BODEGAS
(151 E3) (*ळ F6*)
This spectacular town is nestled away in the narrow gorge of the Río Gua-

A view of the Zahara: the panorama changes with every step you take

dalporcún. Many of the houses have been built into the rock, and only their façades can be seen from the outside. Dominating the surrounding area at the highest point of the town is the ⚜ tower of an old Moorish fort. When it's not locked, you can mount it for a view that extends as far as Olvera. There are INSIDER TIP an incredible number of tapas bars here in Senetil. Two recommendations are *La Tasca (daily | C/ Cuevas del Sol 71 | Tel. 9 56 13 40 24 | Budget)* and the *Restaurante El Mirador (closed Mon | C/ Callejón 10 | Tel. 9 56 13 42 61 | Budget–Moderate)*. Beautifully located on the edge of Ronda is the hotel *El Almendral (28 rooms | Ctra. Setenil, Puerto del Monte at km 0 | tel. 9 56 13 40 29 | www.tugasa.com | Budget)*, with affordable prices and a pool. Information: *Oficina de Turismo (C/ Villa 2 |* tel. 9 56 13 42 61, 6 59 54 66 26 | www. setenildelasbodegas.es)

ZAHARA DE LA SIERRA
(151 D3) (*ɯ F6*)

In Spanish, *zahara* refers to a steep road built on the side of a rocky outcrop. At the top of this muncipality is the Moorish ⚜ *Torre del Homenaje*. The restaurant ⚜ *Al Logo (closed Tue/Wed | C/ Félix Rodríguez de la Fuente 11 | tel. 9 56 12 30 32 | Budget–Moderate)* is on the edge of town and offers a view over the reservoir. Part of the hotel *Arco de la Villa (17 rooms | Camino Nazarí | tel. 9 56 12 32 30 | www. tugasa.com | Budget)* is in the old fortress. Information (e.g. on hiking routes, horseback riding, canoe trips): *Oficina de Información del Parque Natural (Plaza del Rey 3 | tel. 9 56 12 31 14) / www.zaharade lasierra.es, www.zaharacatur.com)*

DISCOVERY TOURS

① ANDALUCÍA AT A GLANCE

START: ① Málaga END: ① Málaga	7 days Driving time: 18 hours
Distance: 🚗 1040 km/646 mi	

COSTS: approx. 250 euros/2 persons
(130 euros for petrol + 60 euros per person for entrance fees and tours) plus accommodation

WHAT TO PACK: Swimwear and sun protection

IMPORTANT TIPS: Before you begin your trip, it's best to book your tickets online for the Alhambra in ④ **Granada** and for a winery tour in ⑪ **Jerez de la Frontera**.

NOTE: The roads in the Serranía de Ronda can get slippery in the winter!

Would you like to explore the places that are unique to this region? Then the Discovery Tours are just the thing for you – they include terrific tips for stops worth making, breathtaking places to visit, selected restaurants and fun activities. It's even easier with the Touring App: download the tour with map and route to your smartphone using the QR Code on pages 2/3 or from the website address in the footer below – and you'll never get lost again even when you're offline.

TOURING APP

→ p. 2/3

Experience the multiple facets of Andalucía on this regional road trip. Starting and ending in Málaga, the tour starts eastwards on the Costa del Sol along the Mediterranean. Next, it spans across Granada, Córdoba and Seville before reaching Cádiz and yet another body of water – the Atlantic. Spain's most southern point and Gibraltar follow after. Finally, it covers the mountain town of Ronda and the seaside resort of Marbella before returning back to Málaga.

The trip begins in the morning from ❶ Málaga → p. 87 and heads east on the A7, a motorway with a seaside view. Walk through ❷ Nerja → p. 94 towards the **Balcón**

DAY 1
❶ Málaga
58 km/36 mi
❷ Nerja

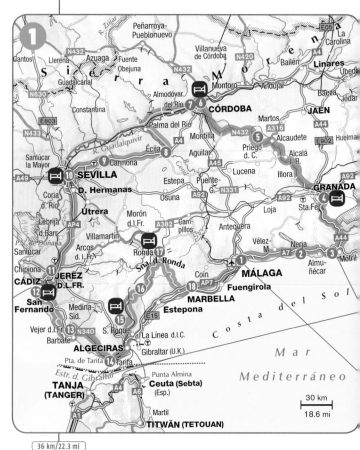

1

Peñarroya-Pueblonuevo · Villanueva de Córdoba · La Carolina · Bailén · Linares · Úbeda · Cantos · Llerena · Azuaga · Fuente Obejuna · Montoro · Andújar · Baeza · Jódar · Guadalcanal · Almodóvar del Río · **CÓRDOBA** · **JAÉN** · Constantina · Palma del Río · Montilla · Martos · Alcaudete · Alcalá l. R. · Huelma · Écija · Aguilar · Priego d. C. · Sanlúcar la Mayor · Carmona · Lucena · Illora · **GRANADA** · **SEVILLA** · Estepa · Puente-G. · Loja · Sta. Fé · D. Hermanas · Osuna · Coria d. Río · Útrera · Morón d.l.Fr. · Cam-pillos · Antequera · Vélez-M. · Nerja · Lebrija d.Barr. · Villamartín · Arcos d. l. Fr. · Ronda · Almu-ñécar · Motril · Sanlúcar · Chipiona · **CÁDIZ** · **JEREZ D.l.Fr.** · Coín · **MÁLAGA** · San Fernando · Medina-Sid. · **MARBELLA** · Fuengirola · Vejer d.l.Fr. · S. Roque · Estepona · Barbate · La Línea d.l.C. · **ALGECIRAS** · Gibraltar (U.K.) · Pta. de Tarifa · Tarifa · Punta Almina · **TANJA (TANGER)** · Ceuta (Sebta) (Esp.) · Martil · **TITWĀN (TETOUAN)**

Costa del Sol · *Mar Mediterráneo*

30 km / 18.6 mi

---

36 km/22.3 mi

3 Salobreña

---

67 km/41.6 mi

4 Granada

---

de Europa, an observation deck with sweeping views over picturesque coves below your feet. Later in **3 Salobreña** → p. 72, walk up the Old Town's steep lanes to reach an Arab **castle**. Then reward yourself by taking a quick dip at the town's beach. **Next, leave the coast near Motril and head north towards Granada. The A 44 runs up past the Alpujarras region and along the foot of the Sierra Nevada before reaching 4 Granada** → p. 64. Spend the afternoon in the city centre and then visit the Moorish district of **Alba-icín**. In the evening, enjoy a flamenco show in a cave in the Sacromonte district. There's also a lovely hotel in the centre at *Plaza Bib-Rambla 22* called **Khü** *(tel. 9 58 22 43 04 | www.khuhotel.com | Moderate)*.

The next morning is dedicated solely to the **Alhambra**. You'll also be able to take in the beauty of this vast palace complex **while driving past the Sierra Subbética towards Córdoba on the N 432**. In the afternoon, take a stop for a light snack or some coffee at the former train station in ❺ **Luque**. There's a popular cantine here where you can stock up on some of the region's delectable olive oil. Where the railway once operated is now a lovely cycle path (68 km/42 mi) called the **Vía Verde de la Subbética** *(www.viasverdes.com)*. Ask the host about renting bikes. Whether you go cycling or not, it's just another hour to ❻ **Córdoba** → p. 36. Once you arrive, book a room at the **Balcón de Córdoba**, where you can take in an evening view of the Guadalquivir. In the morning, visit the **Mezquita**. If you're craving to see more art and culture, satisfy your urge with a visit to the ❼ **Madinat al-Zahra** → p. 42. Here, at these ruins of an old Caliph's palace, you'll uncover more Christian-Muslim history.

Next, get on the A 431 and drive along the Guadalquivir. Once you reach Palma del Río, get on the A 453 and head to ❽ **Écija**, a town nicknamed 'the frying pan of Andalucía' for its scorching-hot summer temperatures. This considered, it may be better to take a pit stop in ❾ **Carmona** → p. 56. Refuel your energy with some authentic tapas and *raciones* at the bar **Mingalario** *(closed Mon/Tue | C/ El Salvador 7 | tel. 9 54 14 38 93 | Budget–Moderate)*. **40 km/25 mi further west on the A 4 you'll reach** ❿ **Seville** → p. 48. Plan to stay the evening, night and next morning here. You'll need time to discover the southern capital of Spain with its magical atmosphere and noteworthy attactions. In the evening, do as the Sevillans do and go tapas-bar hopping. The best place to start is near the cathedral in the **barrio Santa Cruz** or on the **Alameda de Hércules**.

When afternoon temperatures get too hot, jump back in the air-conditioned vehicle and head to ⓫ **Jerez de la Frontera** → p. 83. On the way, take in Andalucía's rolling countryside; pass the vineyards growing from the land's albariza soil, a ground that is white and chalky in nature. These grapes are used to make the region's Sherry, which you'll sample during your **winery tour**. Aren't you happy you booked yours in advance? After the tour, go for tapas in the city centre. Leave Jerez in the late afternoon. **Take the A 4 for 45 minutes** to ⓬ **Cádiz** → p. 76, the oldest city

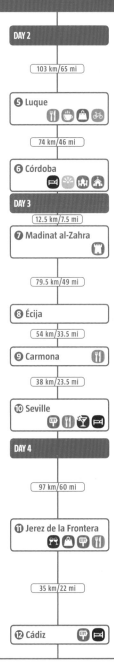

DAY 2

103 km/65 mi

❺ Luque

74 km/46 mi

❻ Córdoba

DAY 3

12.5 km/7.5 mi

❼ Madinat al-Zahra

79.5 km/49 mi

❽ Écija

54 km/33.5 mi

❾ Carmona

38 km/23.5 mi

❿ Seville

DAY 4

97 km/60 mi

⓫ Jerez de la Frontera

35 km/22 mi

⓬ Cádiz

DAY 5

81 km/50 mi

⑬ Vejer de la Frontera

52.5 km/32.5 mi

⑭ Tarifa

49 km/30.5 mi

⑮ Castellar
de la Frontera

DAY 6

50.5 km/31.4 mi

⑯ Gaucín

37.5 km/23.5 mi

⑰ Ronda

DAY 7

62.5 km/39 mi

⑱ Marbella

58 km/36 mi

❶ Málaga

in both Spain and Europe. Located on a promontory in the Atlantic, this city excites visitors with its magical lighting and vibrant Old Town. Stay the night in, e.g. the Old Town's **Hotel La Catedral** *(14 rooms | Plaza de la Catedral 9 | tel. 9 56 29 11 42 | www.hotellacatedral.com | Moderate–Expensive)* and take time to explore the city.

When morning breaks, **explore the coastal roads along the Costa de la Luz that cross Conil and Barbate**. For a quick dip in the ocean, both **El Palmar** near Conil and **Los Caños de Meca** have plenty of long beaches. Continue onwards to the white village of ⑬ **Vejer de la Frontera → p. 83**. From here, you can **get on the N 340**. Stop to visit the sculpture garden **Fundación NMAC → p. 83** and amble through the art. Continue driving to ⑭ **Tarifa → p. 98**, Europe's most southern point. Here you can watch surfers in action and even rent a board yourself. To enjoy an impressive view overlooking the straits and North Africa, go **10 km/6 mi east of Tarifa** to the **Mirador del Estrecho**. Although you may want to visit the Rock of Gibraltar, it's getting too late to properly visit the British exclave. Book a room in the old fortress town of ⑮ **Castellar de la Frontera → p. 100** instead and take time to relax and enjoy its placid beauty.

On today's travel agenda are the south's traditional white villages. First stop is ⑯ **Gaucín → p. 102**, located **along the A 405, a fantastic mountain road**. Next on the list is ⑰ **Ronda → p. 95**. As you approach this city, you'll see why it inspired writers like Ernest Hemingway and Orson Wells. Situated on the top of two cliffs, its breathtaking location, appearance and picturesque ensemble are so unique, that you're going to want to spend an evening and night here. The hotel **Catalonia Reina Victoria** is a good recommendation; Rilke himself even enjoyed his stay.

From Ronda, get on the A 397, another beautiful mountain road that curves its way up the coast. Along the way, stop to visit the chic marina **Puerto Banús**. Follow the excitement with a trip to ⑱ **Marbella → p. 92**; its Old Town is sure to impress with its flower-filled landscaping. For the remainder of the trip, skip the stress of coastal road traffic by **taking the AP 7 toll motorway. From here, ❶ Málaga → p. 87 is about 60 km/37 mi away**. After having travelled an exciting 1000 km/621 mi through the south of Spain, you'll be happy to end your grand tour in this welcoming port city with its many shops and museums.

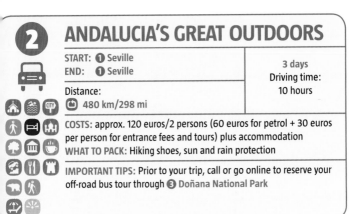

ANDALUCIA'S GREAT OUTDOORS

2

START: ❶ Seville	3 days
END: ❶ Seville	Driving time:
Distance:	10 hours
🚗 480 km/298 mi	

COSTS: approx. 120 euros/2 persons (60 euros for petrol + 30 euros per person for entrance fees and tours) plus accommodation

WHAT TO PACK: Hiking shoes, sun and rain protection

IMPORTANT TIPS: Prior to your trip, call or go online to reserve your off-road bus tour through ❸ Doñana National Park

This road trip starts and ends in Seville and guides you through the lesser-known part of western Andalucía. Explore Doñana National Park, boasting an oasis of wildlife and a landscape filled with dunes and marshes. In the places where Columbus set sail to discover a new world, you'll come across the green Sierra de Aracena and be astounded by its tranquil villages and lovely forests.

Begin by getting on A 49 towards Huelva and leave ❶ Seville → p. 48. Exit onto A 483 and follow the signs marked 'P. N. Doñana'. Drive south through Guadalquivir's flat alluvial landscape. Later, you'll need a much-deserved break. Stop in ❷ El Rocío → p. 45 and drive through the village's sandy roads. Up to a million people come here to visit its pilgrimage church during Pentecost, and many pilgrims come here throughout the year. Just beyond the village is ❸ Doñana National Park → p. 47. **Before you reach the Matalascañas beach resort, turn right and park at the El Acebuche Visitor Centre.** From here, you can hike one of the park's nature trails or take a bus through the national park. In the summer months, these off-road bus tours run from Mon–Sat at 8.30am and 5pm. From mid-September to April, they run from Tue–Sun at 8.30am and 3pm. These tours are the only possible way for you to witness the wildlife in this protected landscape. Later, **continue your journey on A 494 towards ❹ Mazagón → p. 46.** If you feel like visiting a beach, take a break just outside of Mazagón and park in the **Cuesta Maneli car park → p. 46.** From here, you can walk through the dunes of a coastline 13 km/8 mi in length and take a dip in the Atlantic. For the first night, the hotel **Parador de Mazagón** is recommended.

DAY 1

❶ Seville

80.5 km/50 mi

❷ El Rocío 🏠

8 km/4.9 mi

❸ Doñana National Park 🧍🚌🛶🦌🐗

39 km/24.2 mi

❹ Mazagón 🧍🚌🔄🏖️🐗🛏️

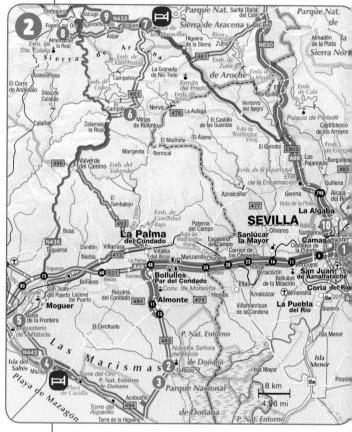

DAY 2

25 km/15.5 mi

5 Palos de la Frontera

107 km/66.4 mi

6 Minas de Riotinto

From Mazagón, continue on A 494 and take A 5026 at the junction to **5 Palos de la Frontera** → p. 46, where people of all ages revel in seeing the replicas of Columbus's ships. In the Friary of **La Rábida**, Columbus convinced the Franciscans to support his exhibition, a step needed for him to approach Queen Isabella for sponsorship. **Next, head north on A 494 to Moguer,** a beautiful whitewashed town where Columbus gathered the sailors who would follow him to the edge of the world. **Then exit onto A 472 towards Niebla,** a town boasting a wall from the Almohad period. **Now head north on A 493 through hilly countryside towards Valverde del Camino. Next, get on N 435 until you reach A 461 and turn right towards 6 Minas de**

Riotinto. From here, you'll pass a stunning mining area. The town isn't beautiful, but the mining museum at **Parque Minero de Riotinto** → p. 126 is nonetheless impressive.

31 km/19.2 mi

The landscape becomes more mountainous and idyllic in Campofrío. **Continue on A 479** to **⑦ Aracena** → p. 32, marked by a striking mountain adorned with a stunning castle and church. For accommodation, the **Los Castaños** *(30 rooms | Av. Huelva 5 | tel. 9 59 12 63 00 | www.loscasta noshotel.com | Budget)* is an affordable recommendation. Anyone who loves good food is sure to like the area surrounding Aracena. The regional *ibérico* ham is an absolute must-try. The area's most exquisite ham is called *Jamón ibérico de Bellota*, a ham leg marked by its dark feet *(patas negras)* and made from black *ibérico* pigs. Bred on *dehesas (a grazing habitat in the Andalucía and Extremadura regions),* the pigs are only fed the acorns *(bellotas)* that grow here during the last phase of their life. More of the Sierra's cuisine can be enjoyed in the region's restaurants, especially INSIDER TIP in autumn during the mushroom and hunting season.

⑦ Aracena

The morning drive **through** the green **Sierra de Aracena** → p. 32 **on HU 8105** is magnificent, but hiking through its chestnut, cork and holm oak forests is even better. From **⑧ Almonaster la Real** → p. 35, there's a hiking trail that leads you to **Cerro de San Cristóbal**, a 917 m/3008 ft-high mountain with a wonderful view over the northern Sierra. Almonaster is one of the most beautiful villages in the re-

DAY 3

27 km/16.7 mi

⑧ Almonaster la Real

The mosque's columned hall in Almonaster la Real

26 km/16 mi

9 Fuenteheridos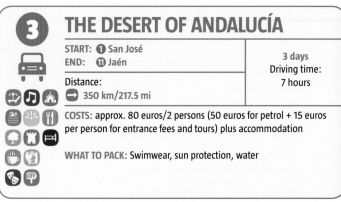

120 km/74.5 mi

10 Itálica

11 km/6.8 mi

1 Seville

gion and boasts a magnificent mosque. After the hike, re-gain your strength with a meal at **Mesón Isabel II** *(closed Tue | C/ Pino 8 | tel. 9 59 14 32 15 | Budget)*. **On the drive back to Aracena**, since you drove past the lovely towns of Alájar and Linares de la Sierra in the morning, **take the route that passes Castaño del Robledo and Fuenteheri-dos**. As beautiful as these whitewashed towns are, why not stop at a Spanish café in **9** **Fuenteheridos** → p. 36?

On the way back to Seville, explore even more of the region by getting off N 433 and onto A 461. While driving, enjoy the view of Zufre, a town perched high in the mountains, and look for the castle above Santa Olal del Cala. Get on **HU 9116 and take the 747 ramp onto A 66**. Heading south, you'll pass **10** **Itálica** → p. 57. Before returning to the 21st century, take an hour to experience these ancient Roman ruins before ending your trip in Andalucía's southern capital of **1** **Seville**.

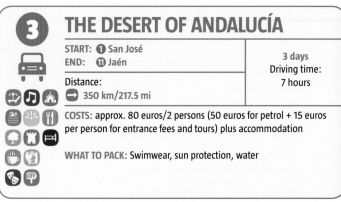

3 THE DESERT OF ANDALUCÍA

START: **1** San José END: **11** Jaén	3 days Driving time: 7 hours
Distance: ➡ 350 km/217.5 mi	

COSTS: approx. 80 euros/2 persons (50 euros for petrol + 15 euros per person for entrance fees and tours) plus accommodation

WHAT TO PACK: Swimwear, sun protection, water

Vast areas of eastern Andalucía are nothing but sand and stone. To make sure you see it all, this road trip begins amidst an old volcanic landscape in the Cabo de Gata Natural Park. From here, you'll cross a desert with towns resembling the Wild West, wind your way up the high plateau of Altiplano de Granada and be astounded by the many cave houses in Guadix. Finally, you'll discover two lovely Renaissance towns placed in the middle of a neverending olive plantation.

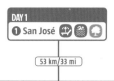

DAY 1
1 San José

53 km/33 mi

Your journey begins in **1** **San José** – the tourist heartland for visiting the **Cabo de Gata Natural Park** → p. 61. Greet the day with a swim in **Playa del Mónsul**. **Next, drive northeast through the region's volcanic landscape.** Take in

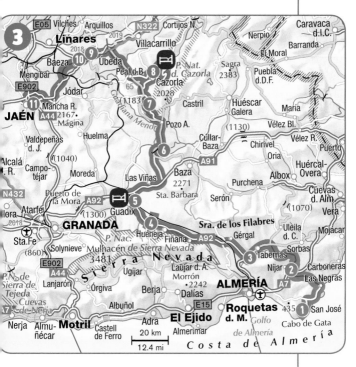

the view of the old Rodalquilar Gold Mine and the massive greenhouses just outside the park. These structures grow vegetables for the supermarkets in middle and northern Europe. Stop for coffee in **❷ Níjar** near the **Iglesia Santa María**. **Head towads N 340a by crossing AL 102, AL 3105 and AL 3103. These mountain roads will give you a view of the only European desert: the Desierto de Tabernas → p. 61. Just before A 92**, you'll reach the western-styled theme park **❸ Oasys**, where some of the biggest names in the Wild West have roamed. Take a while to visit the western town in Mini Hollywood.

On A 92 towards Granada, you'll be spoilt with views across the Sierra de los Filabres and the Sierra Nevada. On your left passing **❹ La Calahorra → p. 72**, you'll see the Castillo de La Calahorra sitting on a foothill against the usually snow-covered backdrop of the Sierra Nevada. Its Renaissance courtyard is a must-see! Not far from La Calahorra along A 92 are plains covered in solar panels; this is

❷ Níjar ☕

49 km/30.4 mi

❸ Oasys 🎡🎵

68.5 km/42.5 mi

❹ La Calahorra 🏛️🏰

33 km/20.5 mi

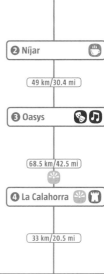

Europe's largest solar power station. Not far from here is tiny INSIDER TIP La Calahorra Railway Station on GR 6103. Film fans, this is where Sergio Leones filmed the famous opening scene to classic western 'Once Upon a Time in the West'.

Back on A 92, drive 17 km/10.5 mi to ❺ **Guadix** → p. 72, a town not only boasting cave houses. Its **cathedral** and the **Plaza de la Constitución** are also worth visiting. Just a short walk away from here is the Old Town's charming **Hotel YIT Abentofail** (30 rooms | C/ Abentofail 8 | tel. 9 58 66 92 81 | www.hotelabentofail.com | Budget–Moderate) with a great restaurant.

Today, you'll be driving through the most scenic part of the journey: the INSIDER TIP Altiplano de Granada. **Get on A 92 N just beyond Guadix and drive 25 km/15.5 mi to El Baúl. Next, take GR 7100 towards Bácor-Olivar.** You'll enjoy a view 1000 m/3281 ft above sea level. The steppe, however, will eventually be dominated by the ❻ **Negratín Reservoir's** glowing turquoise blue waters. Although swimming is prohibited, once you cross the dam, you can enjoy a meal with a view at **Restaurante El Pantano del Negratín** (closed Mon | tel. 9 58 34 22 65 | Budget). After eating, **continue on A 315.** Upon entering the province of Jaén, the landscape will suddenly surround you with olive trees. **In passing Pozo Alcón, get on C 323 towards Quesada. This road winds through pine forests and through** ❼ **Puerto de Tíscar** – in the deep south of the **Sierra de Cazorla.** The view while descending the mountain pass and into a sea of olive groves is simply phenomenal. **Drive through Quesada. From A 315, turn right on A 322. A 319 takes you through** ❽ **Cazorla** → p. 63. Enjoy regional cuisine, relax and stay the night at **Parador de Cazorla** → p. 64.

The last day is a day of culture. From Cazorla, drive through the endless olive groves to ❾ **Úbeda** and ❿ **Baeza** → p. 74, two perfectly preserved Renaissance towns. Finally, in ⓫ **Jaén** → p. 73, visit its **cathedral** and **castle** to overlook the olive trees once more to end the trip on the perfect note.

One of the nearly 66 million olive trees in Jaén

❺ Guadix

DAY 2

46.5 km/289 mi

❻ Negratín Reservoir

43 km/26.7 mi

❼ Puerto de Tíscar

27 km/16.5 mi

❽ Cazorla

DAY 3

94.5 km/58.7 mi

❾ Úbeda

10.5 km/65 mi

❿ Baeza

51 km/31.5 mi

⓫ Jaén

4 BELOW THE SIERRA NEVADA MOUNTAINS

START: ❶ Capileira **END:** ❶ Capileira	**8 hours** Actual walking time: **7 hours**
Distance: 17 km/10.5 mi	**Moderate difficulty** Height: 800 m/2624 ft

COSTS: Estimated travel budget of 20 euros per person for meals
WHAT TO PACK: Hiking shoes, sun and rain protection, water

IMPORTANT TIPS: Avoid going in winter. Wait for good weather, and don't depend on your smartphone since the signal may cut out.

Nestled away in the Sierra Nevada's southern slopes, this moderate hiking trail takes you through the scenic Poqueira valley. You'll discover Alpujarras' spectacular mountain landscape first-hand and visit three picture-perfect villages.

The hiking trail starts in ❶ **Capileira** → p. 72, 1400 m/ 4593 ft above sea level. The trail is located in what is perhaps the most beautiful valley of all the western Alpujarras: the narrow and picturesque **Valle de Poqueira** → **p. 72**. Here you'll see villages tucked away in the slopes of its deep gorge. Up until summer, snow covers the two highest peaks of the Sierra Nevada: the Pico de Veleta (3398 m/11,148 ft) and the Mulhacén (3481 m/11,421 ft), which set the trail's backdrop. Depending on the time of year, it's best to stay the night in a hotel before hiking so you can get an early start. The **Real de Poqueira** (19 rooms | C/ Doctor Castilla 11 | tel. 9 58 76 39 02 | www.hoteles poqueira.es | Budget) is a good recommendation.

08:30am Walk along Calle Castillo in the north of Capileira to an unnamed trail leading to the abandoned village of ❷ **La Cebadilla**. Running along the Río Poqueira, the path is easy to tread and not too wide. Cottonwood trees and bushes grow along the river. As some of the slopes in the valley have been cultivated, they smell of blossoms and herbs in spring. **About an hour and a half into the trail just behind La Cebadilla, you'll cross a small stone bridge and walk along the western side of the valley, which is a lot more narrow.**

From the west flank, you'll be walking in the opposite direction. You'll have to get over a short incline before walk-

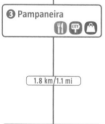

Stop for a midday break in
the whitewashed Pampaneira

ing along the valley's trail. **After roughly 45 minuntes, you'll
cross over the Río Poqueira again via the bridge at Puente
Buchite. Next, you'll cross over the river again with the
Puente de Chiscar. Capileira is now on the other side of the
valley.** The trail isn't always well marked with its red dot, but
it approaches the river again after about an hour in. However, **do not cross the river this time around! Stay on the
western flank and go uphill again. You'll come to a former
mill, and then walk downhill all the way to Pampaneira**.

8.9 km/5.5 mi

❸ Pampaneira

01:00pm Break time! In ❸ **Pampaneira**, rest your legs
and order a meal in the country-style restaurant **Casa Julio**
*(closed Fri | Av. de la Alpujarra 9 | tel. 9 58 76 33 22 | Bud-
get)*. Afterwads, take some time to stroll through the
village. Walk to the Plaza de la Libertad and visit the
17th-century church. Traditional, hand-woven carpets from
Alpujarras are available in the shops.

1.8 km/1.1 mi

❹ Bubión

Next, **walk along the steep Calle Real. Leave the village
and walk along the Camino Real towards ❹ Bubión**. The
trail is easy to find because part of it is on the GR 7 long-
distance footpath, and it's marked with red and white way-
marks. When you reach Bubión, you'll see the village boasts
a regional style of architecture known as *terraos*. These are

simply-built houses with flat roofs. The roofs are protected with *launa*, a mica clay that absorbs moisture.

`03:30pm` **On the way back to Capileira, the trail crosses the valley once more and leads to the bridge ❺ Puente del Molino.** For the remainder of the trip, walk uphill to ❶ **Capileira**. Once you've arrived, regain your strength with a local meal at **Corral del Castaño** *(closed Wed | Plaza del Calvario 16 | tel. 9 58 76 34 14 | Budget–Moderate)*.

1.7 km/1 mi	
❺ Puente del Molino	
1.4 km/0.8 mi	
❶ Capileira	🍴

5 WHITEWASHED VILLAGES & WILD MOUNTAINS

START: ❶ Arcos de la Frontera END: ⓫ Antequera	2 days Driving time: 8 hours
Distance: ➡ 230 km/143 mi	

COSTS: approx. 50 euros/2 persons (40 euros for petrol + 5 euros per person for entrance fees and tours) plus accommodation
WHAT TO PACK: Hiking shoes, rain and sun protection, water

IMPORTANT TIPS: Not for winter or anyone who gets car sick easily. Sign up to hike the Garganta del Chorro in advance!

Steer your way through narrow, curvy roads that wind through the Sierra de Grazalema. From the gorge in El Chorro to the enchanted rocky landschaft in El Torcal, this mountainous region boasts whitewashed villages, art treasures in Antequera and many other unexpected discoveries along the way.

This road trip begins in ❶ **Arcos de la Frontera** → p. 101, a town breathtakingly built on the edge of a vertical cliff. History was written in this valley town 1300 years ago when the Moors won their first battle on the Iberian Peninsula. After taking in the sights, **take A 372 towards the mountains**. In El Bosque, you'll be greeted with a magnificent landscape. Covered with so many beautiful cliffs and forests, it begs you to hike its terrain! Give in and park at the rest area ❷ **Los Llanos del Campo**, 2 km/1.2 mi outside of Benamahoma. The marked hiking trail El Tesorillo, an old charcoal burner's trail, is just 1.2 km/0.75 mi long and leads through a peaceful mountain landscape. If you're lucky, you may get to see black vultures circling the sky.

DAY 1
❶ Arcos de la Frontera

36 km/22 mi

❷ Los Llanos del Campo

13 km/8 mi

3 Grazalema

(15.5 km/9.5 mi)

4 Zahara de la Sierra

DAY 2

(31 km/19. mi)

5 Olvera

(41 km/25.5 mi)

6 Teba

Next, get back on A 372. In **Puerto del Boyar**, the road will incline to 1103 m/3619 ft. Stop at the picturesqe village of **3** Grazalema → p. 102, tucked away in a mountainous valley. Check out the handwoven wool blankets in its charming shops, and go for lunch at one of the restaurants on the Plaza de Andalucía. **After eating, head north on CA 9104 towards Zahara, a narrow road not recommended if you get car sick easily.** Although windy, it crosses stunning mountain passes, the most beautiful of them being **Puerto de las Palomas**. With the road outlining the cliff's edge, you'll be spoilt with phenomenal views. However, if you'd like to avoid the bends and curves, take the longer route on CA 9123. Pass Gaidovar and get on A 2300 towards Zahara, situated above a turquoise-coloured reservoir. Upon arriving in the whitewashed village of **4** Zahara de la Sierra → p. 103, book a room at the hostal **Marqués de Zahara** *(10 rooms | San Juan 3 | tel. 9 56 12 30 61 | www.marquesdezahara.com | Budget)*.

After getting enough rest, make your way to **N 342 towards Olvera. 5** Olvera's white houses are spread over the mountain like sprinkled sugar. In the town, you'll find a castle and church that is near a bar with a fantastic view over the landscape, Bar **El Tapir Despistado** *(closed Mon–Wed | Plaza Torre del Pan 1)*. **Continue east on A 384 for 25 km/15.5 mi and take MA 467 to 6** Teba, where the Battle of Teba took place next to the INSIDERTIP **Castillo de la Estrella** in 1330. There's a small museum in the cas-

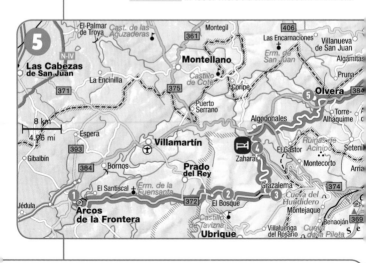

tle's keep about the fighting between the Nasrid dynasty and the Castilians. The castle also offers an amazing view over the highland region.

Continue driving south. Before reaching Ardales, drive north on MA 5403 past the ❼ Embalse del Conde de Guadalhorce, a turquoise-green reservoir that almost looks surreal under the summer sun. **Park the car at the 'Los Eucaliptos' car park.** From here, you can go for a swim or rent a canoe. **After passing the excavation site in Bobastro, you'll hit a curvy road that winds into the village ❽ El Chorro**. Take the exit towards **Garganta del Chorro → p. 91**. Boasting a narrow gorge with cliffs 200 m/656 ft in height, this place is a major hub for rock climbers. Other can cross the **Caminito del Rey** to experience these heights. Since reopening, the masses have rushed here to see this one-of-a-kind walkway.

Make your way to MA 4401 towards Valle de Abdalajís and continue towards Antequera. Visit the wolf park **❾ Lobo Park Antequera → p. 127** on the way. **Continue towards Antequera.** Although this is your final destination, you'll initially pass it and take a detour to the natural park **❿ Paraje Natural El Torcal → p. 91**. Its rocky landscape is simply incredible and offers sweeping views 1100 m/ 3609 ft above sea level. They are most beautifully lighted in the early evening. Finally, after enjoying the nature, drive back to **⓫ Antequera → p. 91**, where you can book a room.

26 km/16 mi

❼ Embalse del Conde de Guadalhorce

8 km/5 mi

❽ El Chorro

25 km/15.5 mi

❾ Lobo Park Antequera

20 km/12.4 mi

❿ Paraje Natural El Torcal

16 km/10 mi

⓫ Antequera

SPORTS & ACTIVITIES

Andalucía's varied countryside provides a variety of possibilities for active holiday-goers. Go golfing year-round, skiing in the Sierra Nevada, hiking, cycling in the natural parks or do water sports in the Atlantic and Mediterranean.

The south is known worldwide for its golf courses and Taria's surfing spots. The densely forested Sierra de Aracena is perfect for hiking. Even for many Spaniards, the mountainous Sierra Morena, north of Córdoba, remains unknown territory. In the northeast, the Sierra de Cazorla, Segura y las Villas Natural Park is Spain's largest protected area. Horseback riding, climbing and canyoning are popular here. Active holiday-goers may see the vultures or eagles living here while hiking or cycling through the area. The de-sert-like region around Cabo de Gata is also sure to fascinate nature enthusiasts.

CLIMBING

Rock climbing is popular in Andalucía. Climbing fans from around the world travel to Málaga's backcountry to climb the Caminito del Rey in Garganta del Chorro. There are interesting climbing areas near Tarifa in the Sierra de San Bartolomé and in Grazalema. Find a climbing school at *www.escuelasdeescalada.com* (website only in Spanish).

CYCLING

The old railway lines of the *Vías Verdes* have since been turned into cycle and

Photo: A beach horseback ride in Matalascañas on the Costa de la Luz

Despite the season, water and wind surfers, mountain bikers, hikers and golfers can all pursue their passion here in Andalucía!

hiking paths that go across old bridges and through tunnels (currently 29 routes, information on bike rentals and routes: *www.viasverdes.com*). When ski season ends, mountain bikers can ride the trails and lifts in the *Sierra Nevada Bike Park* (*www.sierranevada.es*). The *Transandalus* (*www.transandalus.org*), a 2000 km/ 1242 mi-long mountain bike route, is also good fun. It circles all of Andalucía, crossing over many of its unique nature parks. To survive the route, however, you'll have to have a navigation system, since it isn't

marked. To know where to go, download the GPS routes for free online. Organised bike tours can be booked, e.g. at *Almería Bike Tours* (*tel. 9 50 31 73 00 | www. almeria-bike-tours.com*) in Almería or *Camaleón Sports* (*tel. 6 39 43 14 64 | www. camaleonsports.de*) in Conil.

DIVING

Diving into the Mediterranean and Atlantic is possible from a number of different coastlines. Located between Carboneras and Cabo de Gata, the undersea world in INSIDER TIP Marine Natural Park is particularly impressive. Experienced divers are especially impressed with the underwater shipwrecks in the Strait of Gibraltar. Diving in the waters around Nerja is also interesting. Some recommeded diving centres include *Isub (San José | C/ Babor 3 | tel. 9 50 38 00 04 | www.isub sanjose.com)* in Cabo de Gata Natural Park; *Buceo Costa Nerja (Playa Burriana | tel. 9 52 52 86 10 | www.nerjadiving.com)* in Nerja on the Costa del Sol; and *Happy Diver's Club (Atalaya Park Hotel | Ctra. de Cádiz at km 168.5 | tel. 6 09 57 19 20 | www.happy-divers-marbella.com)* in Estepona.

GOLF

The Costa del Sol is the only place in Europe where so many golf courses are concentrated in an area this small. On the coast's motorway, you'll see huge signs every few kilometres reading 'Costa del Sol – Costa del Golf'. But other places on the coast and further inland are trying to woo golf-lovers, too. Andalucía has around 140 golf clubs, including the most famous of all Spanish courses – the *Valderrama (www.valderrama.com)*, located between Castellar de la Frontera and Gibraltar in Sotogrande. Gather information on courses and green requirements at *Federación Andaluza de Golf (tel. 9 52 22 55 90 | www.rfga.org)* or online at *www.golfinspain.com.*

HIKING

For maps or suggested hiking routes, visit the *centros de interpretación*. Many of the paths are either poorly marked or not marked at all.
– Sierra de Aracena: *Plaza Alta | Aracena | tel. 9 59 12 95 53 | sierradearacena.com*

– Sierra de Grazalema: *Av. de la Diputación 1 | El Bosque | tel. 9 56 70 97 33 | turismograzalema.com;* in Grazalema, *Horizón (C/ Las Piedras 1 | tel. 9 56 13 23 63 | www.horizonaventura.com)* offers a number of hiking trails and outdoor activities (website only in Spanish)
– Sierra Nevada: *(Ctra. de la Sierra Nevada, km 23 | Güéjar Sierra | Tel. 9 58 34 06 25 | cveldornajo.blogspot.com)*

HORSEBACK RIDING

Countless stables *(picaderos)* offer guided horseback rides. They go along the coast, across bull-grazing pastures and through nature parks. They can last anywhere from a few hours to several days and include accommodation. Horseback riding holidays can be booked, e.g. at *In the Saddle (www.inthesaddle.com)* or *www.unicorntrails.com.* The Swiss veterinarian Christina Ward also offers horseback rides across the beaches of Tarifa and in the natural park of Los Alcornocales. For booking, contact *Aventura Ecuestre (Hotel Dos Mares | Tarifa | tel. 9 56 23 66 32 | www.aventuraecuestre. com).* Located in Mijas, *Rancho La Paz (Torreblanca del Sol | Fuengirola | tel. 9 52 59 02 64 | www.ranchopaz.alfahosting. org)* also offers beach horseback rides. Multi-day tours across the Serranía de Ronda and Atlantic coastline are also available.

SKIING

The Sierra Nevada is Europe's most southern skiing area, boasting 124 ski runs that cover 107 km/66 mi. A heavenly ski resort is *Pradollano (ski pass from 41 euros | www.sierranevada.es).* It's open at weekends from December to April and is easy to reach by car. The ski runs are over 2000 m/1245 ft high.

WATER SPORTS

Tarifa is one of the best places to go surfing in Europe. The Strait of Gibraltar acts as a wind tunnel, making it ideal for the experienced wind and kite surfers. You'll find many surfing centres northwest of Tarifa along N 340 and on the beaches towards Punta Paloma. These include *Spin Out (Ctra. Cádiz, km 75.5 | tel. 9 56 23 63 52 | www.tarifaspinout.com)* and *Escuela Dos Mares (Ctra. Cádiz, at km 79.5 | tel. 9 56 68 40 35 | www.escueladosmares. com)*. Those who prefer a lighter breeze should surf the Mediterranean. For wind surfing, Roquetas de Mar on the Costa de Almería offers the most activities. El Palmar in Conil is ideal for wave surfing. Tarifa, Marbella, Roquetas and El Palmar are perfect for stand-up paddling.

WELLNESS

If you're looking for great spas and spa activities, you'll find most of them in recently-built hotel facilities.

Andalucía has a long tradition in thalassotherapy. With its abundance of seawater, salty air, sun and sand, the region has all the 'raw materials' needed for this therapy to improve your health. Spend time relaxing in the 47-degree hot springs in Alhama de Granada *(www.balnearioalhamadegranada.com)*. They've been in use since ancient Rome. Immerse yourself in the calming environment associated with the old Arab bathing culture by visiting the hamams of Málaga, Granada and Córdoba *(www.hammam alandalus.com)*. Your health will thank you for it.

The mountain hiking trails are especially scenic in the region's natural and national parks

TRAVEL WITH KIDS

Andalucíans like children a lot. It's common for strangers to greet them with hugs, especially the small ones! And the parents don't even bat an eyelid.

You're not going to have any problems travelling with children in Andalucía, a region offering plenty of childrens' activities. Children are very much a part of Spain's everyday life. Even if it's past midnight, it's common to see children playing during the summer months.

In the areas heavily visited by tourists, Andalucía has developed a number of recreational activities in recent years that are suited for families with children of all ages. Even when seeing the wonders coming out of the Moorish era, children experience these places with just the astonishment that you do.

THE WEST

ACUARIO DE SEVILLA ●
(145 E4) (*m* D4)

Around 7000 sea creatures live in 31 tanks in the aquarium on the southern end of Maria Luisa Park. The amount of life frolicing throughout the Guadalquivir, Atlantic and Pacific is incredible, like the lurking sharks with their elegant movements. Or the Sevillians' favourite, the two mating turtles! With their help, the aquarium plans to resettle turtles in the Cabo de Gata-Níjar Natural Park. *Sept–June Mo–Thu 10am–7pm, Fr–Sun 10am–8pm, July/Aug Mon–Thu 11am–20pm, Fri–Sun 11am–9pm | admission 15 euros, children under 14 years 10 euros | Muelle de las Delicias | www.acuariosevilla.es*

**Andalucíans are child-friendly and uncompli-
cated – they take their children everywhere
and let them stay up until late**

AQUOPOLIS SEVILLA (145 E4) (*Ø D4*)
A massive water park in the east of the
city with lots of attractions. Bus line
55 stops right outside. *2nd half of June
daily 12pm–7pm, July/Aug 12pm–8pm |
admission 22 euros, children under
1.40 m/4.6 ft 16 euros, reduced prices online at www.sevilla.aquopolis.es*

COTO DE DOÑANA
(145 D5–6) (*Ø C5–6*)
Take an off-road tour through the national park and watch wild horses, boars,
deer and waterbirds roam freely. The
landscape is amazing. (*May–mid-Sept
Mon–Sat 8.30am and 5pm, mid-Sept–Ap-
ril Tue–Sun 8.30am and 3pm | 30 euros |
tel. 9 59 43 04 32 | www.donanavisitas.
es*). The boat trip from Sanlúcar de Barrameda through the Doñana is also nice.
Combine the boat tour with the off-road
tour for more excitement: *Centro de Visitantes Fábrica de Hielo (daily 10am, April/
May/Oct also 4pm, June–Sept also 5pm |
17.50 euros | Av. Bajo de Guia | tel. 9 56
36 38 13 | www.visitasdonana.com)*

Everyone's fav! The wave slide Pistas Blandas is a real crowd-pleaser at Aquamijas

ISLA MÁGICA (145 E4) (*ØD D4*)

You'll have a blast conquering the roller-coasters at this theme park, located on the grounds of the former Expo World's Fair. *Opening times vary, see website | day ticket 29 euros, children (5–12 yrs.) 21 euros | www.islamagica.es*

MUELLE DE LAS CARABELAS
(144 B4) (*ØD B5*)

A museum boasting true-to-original replicas of the three ships used by Christopher Columbus and his crew to find a route to India in 1492. It's located in La Rábida at the mouth of the Río Tinto. *Mid-June–mid-Sept Tue–Sun 10am–8pm, mid-Sept–mid-June 9.30am–7.30pm | admission 3.55 euros, families 7.45 euros*

INSIDER TIP ▶ PARQUE MINERO
DE RIOTINTO (144 C3) (*ØD C3*)

Metal ore has been mined on the Río Tinto in Huelva province for thousands of years. The area's mining history is told in

the *museum (daily 10.30am–3pm, 4pm–7pm, Aug till 8pm | admission 5 euros, children (4–12 yrs.) 4 euros | Plaza Ernest Lluch)* in Minas de Riotinto. For a more exciting adventure, book a ride on Spain's oldest steam locomotive as it travels through a crater landscape. Tickets *(from 11 euros, children from 10 euros)* are available in the museum.

THE EAST

AQUA TROPIC (153 E5) (*ØD K6*)

A fun water park on Almuñécar beach. *Mid-June–Sept daily 11am–7pm | admission 21 euros, junior (12–15 yrs.) 16 euros, children (4–11 yrs.) 15 euros | Paseo Marítimo (Playa de Velilla) | www.aqua-tropic. com*

PARQUE DE LAS CIENCIAS ●
(153 E3) (*ØD K5*)

This science centre in Granada is Andalucía's most visited museum. Topics presented include the universe and perception. The museum offers interactive experiments and a special area for 3–7- year-olds. *Tue–Sat 10am–7pm, Sun 10am–3pm | admission 7 euros, children 6 euros, Planetarium 2.50 euros, children 2 euros | Av. de la Ciencia | www.parqueciencias.com*

SIERRA NEVADA (153 E–F4) (*M K5*)

Summer fun for the whole family! Slide downhill in a toboggan at 40 km/h/ 25 mph *(4.50 euros/ride)*. Other activities include archery practice and riding a fat-tire scooter downhill. *Mirlo Blanco in the Pradollano ski resort | sierranevada.es*

THE SOUTH

AQUAMIJAS (152 B6) (*M G7*)

A fantastic water park in Fuengirola. *Mid-April–May daily 10.30am–5.30pm, June and 1st half of Sept 10.30am–6pm, 2nd half of Sept 10.30am–5.30pm, July/Aug 10am–7pm | admission 25, 8–12 years 19 euros, 3–7 years 14 euros, reduced prices online | A 7 at km 209 | www.aquamijas.com*

CROCODILE PARK (152 B6) (*M H6–7*)

400 crocs! Some just hatched; others are 4 m/13 ft long. *Daily 11am–5pm, May/June and Oct till 6pm, July–Sept till 7pm | admission 16 euros, 5–10 years 12 euros, 3–4 years 6 euros, reduced prices online | Torremolinos | C/ Cuba 14 | www.cocodrilospark.com*

LOBO PARK ANTEQUERA (152 B4) (*M G5*)

Take a guided tour through an enclosed wolf park. Tours are offered during the day and in the evening. *Thu–Tue 11am, 1pm, 3pm and 4.30pm | admission 11 euros, children under 12 years 7 euros | A 343 Antequera, Álora at km 16 | www.lobopark.com*

MUSEO ALBORANIA (152 B–C5) (*M H6*)

A museum and seawater aquarium on the port of Málaga. *July–mid-Sept daily 11am–2pm and 5pm–8pm, mid-Sept–June 10.30am–2pm and 4.30pm–6.30pm | admission 7 euros, children (4–17 yrs.) 5 euros | Palmeral de las Sorpresas | museoalborania.com*

SEA LIFE BENALMÁDENA (152 B6) (*M H7*)

A lovely underwater zoo, perfect for small children who love seahorses. *Daily 10am–8.30pm | admission 16 euros, children (3–9 yrs.) 13 euros | reduced prices online | Puerto Deportivo Benalmádena | www.visitsealife.com*

SELWO AVENTURA (151 E4) (*M F7*)

This adventure park in Estepona is a zoo with animal shows. Children love it! *Feb–April and Sept–Nov daily 10am–6pm, May/June 10am–7pm, July/Aug 10am–8pm | admission 24.90 euros, children (3–10 yrs.) 17 euros, reduced prices online | A 7 at km 162.5 | www.selwo.es*

SELWO MARINA (152 B6) (*M H7*)

A water park in Benalmádena on the Costa del Sol. The biggest attraction hands down is the amazing dolphin show! *Show times vary, see website | admission 19.90 euros, children (3–10 yrs.) 15 euros, reduced prices online | Parque de la Paloma Benalmádena | selwomarina.es*

WHALE WATCHING (151 D6) (*M E8*)

The Strait of Gibraltar is an important waterway not only for ships, but also for dolphins and whales. Wildlife-watching tours from Taria are offered by *Whale Watch Taria (www.whalewatchtarifa.net)* and by *Firmm (www.firmm.org)*. *Price approx. 30–50 euros, children approx. 20–30 euros*

FESTIVALS & EVENTS

The most famous festivals in Andalucía are religious. Those who've experienced the Semana Santa or the pilgrimage to El Rocío come to know how deeply devout the Andalucíans are. But even more than the Virgin Mary or the Son of God, the Andalucíans love celebrating life itself. No matter the festival, it makes for a good reason to put on your finest clothes, have your hair cut or just style it fancily with gel or hairspray.

FESTIVALS AND EVENTS

FEBRUARY

The *Carnival of Cádiz* is the most famous festival in Spain and lasts until the Sunday after Ash Wednesday. *www.carnavalde cadiz.com*

FEBRUARY/MARCH

⭐ *Festia de Jerez*: A two-week-long flamenco festival featuring the biggest artists in the scene. *www.festivaldejerez.es*

MARCH/APRIL

The ⭐ ● *Semana Santa* (Holy Week) in Andalucía is celebrated with processions. Although the most famous and spectacular one is in Seville, the processions in Granada, Córdoba, Málaga, Úbeda and Jaén are also worth seeing. The peak of this festival takes place on the night before Good Friday.

⭐ *Feria de Abril:* A week-long April market eight days after Easter in Seville and the biggest festival in Andalucía. Carriages, elegant equestrians and women in costume all fill the streets.

Málaga Film Festival: The biggest Spanish film festival. *www.festivaldemalaga. com*

MAY

Cruces de Mayo: In the first week of May, locals brightly decorate crosses and present them in many of the region's towns and cities.

Spanish Grand Prix: A motorbike race in Jerez and a massive festival for bikers *www.circuitodejerez.com*

Feria del Caballo: This is the horse market in Jerez and the city's biggest festival. INSIDER TIP ▶ *Festival de los Patios Cordobeses:* A competition to have Córdoba's most beautiful patio.

PENTACOST

⭐ *Pilgrimage to El Rocío:* Hundreds of thousands of pilgrims, some on horseback, make their way to the 'Virgin of the Dew' in El Rocío.

Life is beautiful! Whether it's a secular or religious festival, Andalucíans especially love to celebrate who they are

JUNE/JULY

Fiesta de San Juan – 24 June: A firework show to celebrate Saint John's Eve.

Festival Internacional de Música y Danza de Granada: An important festival for classical to contemporary music and ballet. *www.granadafestival.org*

Festival de la Cueva: Ballet, music and operas performed in the caves of Nerja at the end of July. *www.cuevadenerja.es*

AUGUST

INSIDER TIP *Carreras de Caballo de Sanlúcar de Barrameda:* The 'Sanlúcar Horse Race' on the sandy banks of the Guadalquivir. *www.carrerassanlucar.es*

SEPTEMBER

Feria de Pedro Romero: Bullfighting festival in Ronda. *www.turismoderonda.es*

NOVEMBER

Festival de Jazz de Granada: An important European jazz festival. *www.jazz granada.es*

NATIONAL HOLIDAYS

Public holidays falling on Sunday are usually pushed to Monday.

Jan 1	Año Nuevo
Jan 6	Reyes Magos
Feb 28	Día de Andalucía
March/April	Maundy Thursday (Jueves Santo)
March/April	Good Friday (Viernes Santo)
May 1	Día del Trabajo
Aug 15	Asunción de Nuestra Señora
Oct 12	Columbus Day (Día de la Hispanidad)
Nov 1	Todos los Santos
Dec 6	Constitution Day (Día de la Constitución)
Dec 8	Immaculate Conception (Inmaculada Concepción)
Dec 25	Navidad

LINKS, BLOGS, APPS & MORE

LINKS & BLOGS

www.andalucia.org/en/ Everything you ever wanted to know about holidaying in Andalucía, with news, tips, planning tips, destinations, an events calendar, interactive maps. etc.

www.iberianature.com/directory/adventure-sports-and-outdoor-activities-in-spain/hiking-in-spain/hiking-in-andalucia/ A useful guide to hikes in the mountains and parks in western Andalucía, whether you're with a group or on your own.

www.andalucia.com/province/home.htm With all sorts of information, also for those planning to settle in the region.

blog.andalucia.com You name it, you'll find it here. Anything vaguely related to the Andalucían experience is commented on here for all to read.

andaluciablog.blogspot.com News in English about all things Andalucían as well as useful tips.

www.expat-blog.com Enter 'Andalucía' and off you go! Ideal for anyone wanting to work, live or move to Andalucía. Or simply for those wanting to find out about life in the far south. These blogs are written by expats living in the region.

twitter.com/sevillaciudad Everything that's going on in Andalucía's capital can be found here in the typical brief twitter manner in English and Spanish.

www.facebook.com/costadelsolspain With some 18,500 Costa del Sol fans who are just dying to show you their holidy snaps and anything else that could interest sun-worshippers on the coast.

www.facebook.com/Andalucía Typical site for Andalucía fans.

twitter.com/viveandalucia With all sorts of details about sports events, concerts, news and culture. Many things are shown in real-time via the Andalucía ticker in Spanish.

Regardless of whether you are still researching your trip or already in Andalucía: these addresses will provide you with more information, videos and networks to make your holiday even more enjoyable

www.youtube.com/watch?v=Bjt2ynb84ok Flamenco dancing in the streets of Seville showing the spontaneity and pure pleasure of dancing. With links to all sorts of related videos.

uk.video.search.yahoo.com/search/video?p=andalucia+video+alhambra A wide selection of videos to give you an idea of the magnificence of the Alhambra in Granada.

uk.video.search.yahoo.com/search/video?p=andalucia+video+national+parks Another wide selection of videos that will take you on a virtual tour around some of Andalucía's national and natural parks.

www.youtube.com/watch?v=JYQIQaP2lSY An interesting report on the pilgrimage in El Rocío. The report gives a good impression of the devout procession and has English subtitles, too.

canalflamenco.radio.de While listening to the flamenco music on this online radio station, try to guess what colour the music reminds you of.

www.spain-holiday.com/Granada-city A five-minute clip on Granada.

Seville With there being so many highlights in Seville, it would be impossible to name them all in this travel guide. This app from the tourist information office, however, allows you to see it all in the palm of your hand.

Beaches App Costa del Sol This app lists all the beaches on the Costa del Sol and provides the user with information on the area's shops, bars, events, etc.

Spain Newspapers If you can speak a bit of Spanish, this app provides you with a practical list of all of Spain's biggest newspapers. These include, for example, El País, El Mundo, ABC, Diario de Seville and, of course, Marca, the daily sports newspaper.

TRAVEL TIPS

ARRIVAL

✈ The most important airport in Andalucía is in Málaga (AGP airport, www.aeropuertodemalagacostadelsol.com). It is just 10 km/6.2 mi west of the city centre. This is where holiday-makers land who are staying on the Costa del Sol or Costa Tropical. The airport has the best transportation infrastructure to get you where you need. There are good bus and train connections here and familiar car hire companies. For 1.80 euros, the C1 local train line (short.travel/and6) to either the city centre or Torremolinos and Fuengirola is ten minutes.

For those travelling to east Andalucía, Almería is just 10 km/6.2 mi from the city centre. The airport in Granada (GRX, www.aena.es) is 20 km/12.4 mi from the city centre, but there aren't many direct flights from abroad. The airports in Jerez de la Frontera (XRY, www.aena.es) and Seville (SVQ, www.sevilla-airport.com) are perfect for holiday-goers aiming to visit Costa de la Luz. Both airports are 10 km/6.2 mi from the city centre. The flights from England to Andalucía are 3–6 hours. Other airports include Faro in Portugal (approx. 70 km/44 mi from west Andalucía) and Madrid (approx. 300 km/186 mi from north Andalucía). From Madrid, take the AVE high-speed train (www.renfe.com). It will take you to Seville or Córdoba in 2–3 hours. Roundtrip tickets start at 75 euros. Iberia and Renfe offer cheap combination tickets. For more information on each airline, visit the Spanish airport portal at *www.aena.es*.

🚗 Andalucía is far away from the UK. Allow 2.5–3 days to drive to Spain. From London to Almería, it is 2300 km/1500 mi. The most direct route is via Paris, Marseille and Barcelona. Others take the ferry from Portsmouth or Plymouth to Santander or Bilbao and then drive down across the country. Route planners are available online and help calculate the cost of the trip, including toll fees for the motorways in France and Spain.

🚆🚌 Travelling by train can take up to 30 hours and involves several changes. The cost is generally higher than a plane ticket. For more information, see: *www.renfe.com* and *www.seat61.com*

CAMPING

Information on the more than 100 campsites in Andalucía can be obtained from the *Federación Andaluza de Campings* (www.andaluciacampings.com) or under *www.campingsonline.com*.

RESPONSIBLE TRAVEL

It doesn't take a lot to be environmentally friendly whilst travelling. You should think not only about your carbon footprint whilst flying to and from your holiday destination, but also about how you can protect nature and culture abroad. As a tourist, it is especially important to respect the environment, buy more local products, replace driving with cycling, save water and much more. If you'd like to find out more about eco-tourism, please visit *www.ecotourism.org*.

From arrival to weather

Your holiday from start to finish: the most important addresses and information for your trip to Andalucía

CAR HIRE

Depending on the season and model, a car hire costs 25 euros a day and up. Look for a car hire with high coverage, unlimited kilometres, no deductible, a good fuel policy (preferably the full-full option) and perhaps low costs for a second driver. It's also important to know where the station is. It's most convenient to rent and return the car at the airport to spare you any stress on the day you leave; the shuttle bus sometimes runs late between the rental station and airport. To compare prices, book a car hire or, for more information, go to *www.easycar.com, www.expedia.co.uk* or *www.carrentals.co.uk*.

CLIMATE & WHEN TO TRAVEL

Spring and autumn are the most pleasant times of year in Andalucía. At the peak of summer, you will have to deal with searing heat; the nights, however, are balmy. The Spanish school holidays are from July to the beginning of September, between Christmas and January 6th and during Semana Santa. It's difficult to find last-minute accommodation during this time. The sea's temperature is pleasent from May/June to mid-November. Winters are cool and sometimes wet. Expect it to be cold and snowy near the mountains. The main attractions are less crowded in winter.

CONSULATES & EMBASSIES

BRITISH CONSULATE
Edificio Eurocom | C/ Mauriccio Moro Pareto 2 | 29006 Málaga | tel. 9 02 10 93 56 | www.ukinspain.fco.gov.uk

BUDGETING

Taxi	£1.25/$1.75	*per kilometre by day in Málaga, Mo–Fri*
Coffee	£0.90– £1.75/$1.20–$2.50	*for a 'café solo' at the counter*
Snack	around £5/$7	*for a bowl of gazpacho*
Wine	£1.70–£2.60/$2.46–$3.70	*for a glass of wine at the bar*
Petrol	around £1.20/$1.70	*for 1 litre (super)*
Sunbed	around £7.90/$11	*to rent for one day*

CONSULATE OF THE UNITED STATES OF AMERICA
Edificio Lucio 1°-C | Av Juan Gómez Juanito 8 | 29640 Fuengirola | tel. 9 52 47 48 91 | madrid.usembassy.gov

CONSULATE OF CANADA
Plaza de la Malagueta 2, 1° | 29016 Málaga | tel. 9 52 22 33 46 | www.canada international.gc.ca

CUSTOMS

For EU citizens, the following duty-free allowances apply (import and export): for one's own consumption, 800 cigarettes, 400 cigarillos, 200 cigars, 1 kg tobacco, 20 L aperitif, 90 L wine (with a maximum amount of 60 L sparkling wine) and 110 L beer. Travellers to the US who are residents of the country do not have to pay duty on articles purchased overseas up to the value of $800, but there are limits on the number of alcoholic beverages and tobacco products. For the regulations for international travel for US residents, please see www.cbp.gov

DRIVING

The Andalucían road network has been profoundly expanded. Motorways now link all provincial capitals, and gaps are being filled in bit by bit. There are a few toll motorways in Andalucía – these are marked 'AP' *(autopista de peaje)*. The toll-free motorways are abbreviated with 'A' *(autovía)*. The national and provincial roads are all in good condition.

The speed limit permitted in built-up areas is 50 km/h/30 mph; 90 km/h/55 mph on country roads and 120 km/h/75 mph for motorways.

The legal drink-driving limit is a blood alcohol level of 0.5 mg per ml. It's illegal to have your lights on or talk on the phone while fuelling. Car rentals must be equipped with two warning triangles. In case of a breakdown, place them in front of and behind the vehicle and put on a high-visibility vest. These things must be in the car whilst travelling. For breakdown service, call the automobile club RACE at *tel. 9 00 11 22 22*.

ELECTRICITY

The standard voltage is Spain is 230 V. You may need to buy a Spanish travel adaptor.

EMERGENCY SERVICES

Emergency no. for police, fire brigade and other emergency services: *tel. 112*

ENTERING SPAIN

EU cititzens travelling to Spain will need a valid ID or a children's ID (up until 16 yrs. old). Minors travelling on their own will also need to gain permission from their caretaker. You will otherwise need a valid passport – even though it is no longer checked on immigration from Schengen countries – and you should have it on you at all times in case of police checks (for motorists), reporting a theft, etc. Tourists from the US, Canada and Australia do not need a visa for stays under 90 days. Border controls in Gibraltar may take some time, however.

HEALTH

If you urgently need to see a doctor, request an A&E *(urgencia)* from your nearest hospital, but expect a long wait in the process. The Spanish health system is medically up-to-date but generally overburdened. If you have a European Health Insurance Card (EHIC), look on the back to see if you're entitled to free treatment in state hospitals and from doctors registered with the Servicio Andaluz de Salud (SAS). If you're treated at a private practice or clinic, you'll be expected to pay on the spot. In such cases, it may be worth it to get travel health insurance prior to your holiday. Pharmacies *(farmacias)* can be found everywhere in Spain, and some medicine can be obtained without a prescription. It may even be cheaper than back home.

INFORMATION

SPANISH TOURIST OFFICE TURESPAÑA
- *64 North Row | W1K 7DE, London | tel. 020 7317 2011 | www.spain.info*
- *845 North Michigan Av, Suite 915-E | Chicago IL 60611 | tel. 312 642 1992 | www.spain.info/en_US*
- *20 East 42nd Street, Suite 5300 | New York NY 10165-0039 | tel. 216 265 8822 | www.spain.info/en_US*

INFORMATIONAL WEBSITES
www.spain.info, www.andalucia.org

INTERNET CAFÉS & WIFI

WiFi is available for free in most hotels and *hostales*. There's usually a good connection in the historical buildings, but some are too old for a good connection. Public WiFi is often available in the reception area of many buildings. Bars and restaurants offering an internet hotspot are commonly marked with a black-and-white WiFi sticker. If you're travelling without a smartphone, tablet or laptop, ask around where you might find a *locutorio*. Here you can use a computer, pay per minute or hour to go online and make cheap calls abroad.

MONEY & PRICES

Andalucía is still cheaper than England. Money can be obtained from cash dispensers everywhere using an EC card. Credit cards are accepted in hotels, shops and restaurants, but not necessarily in taxis or hostels/guesthouses.

Admission prices for the museums and tourist attractions depend on their popularity. It's common for there to be discount prices for children, students and retirees. Some museums offer free entry to the museum once a week – sometimes for the whole day, other times after a certain time of day. Many cities offer a visitor's card for reduced fares. Buying one, however, is only worth it if you plan on seeing many of the cultural sites.

NATURISM

Nudism is allowed in Spain, but it's not that widespread. Although going topless is tolerated, being completely nude is only allowed on a few specifically marked beaches *(playas naturistas)* and on isolated bays, like the one in Cabo de Gata.

OPENING HOURS

The shops in Spain are allowed to open and close when they please. In most cases, from Monday to Friday, they open at 9.30am or 10am. The shops close for a break at 1.30pm or 2pm and open up again at 4.30pm or 5pm. Closing time is usually at 8pm. Sometimes on Saturday they only stay open in the morning. Businesses in holiday destinations, however, will stay open all day and late into the night. Although the opening hours listed in this guidebook have been carefully researched, be aware that the opening times of the tourist attractions and museums change frequently. Tourist information

CURRENCY CONVERTER

£	€	€	£
1	1.15	1	0.85
3	3.40	3	2.65
5	5.70	5	4.40
13	17.70	13	11.50
40	45	40	35
75	85	75	66
120	136	120	106
250	283	250	220
500	565	500	440

$	€	€	$
1	0.80	1	1.20
3	2.40	3	3.70
5	4	5	6.20
13	10.50	13	16
40	32.50	40	50
75	60	75	92
120	97	120	148
250	200	250	310
500	405	500	615

For current exchange rates, see www.xe.com

offices should know the up-to-date times. Restaurants also frequently change their opening times and closed days. So, if you want to make sure, give them a ring first.

PETS

Generally speaking, when travelling with an animal, it has to be issued a certificate by a veterinarian or get a pet passport. Dogs and cats have to be inoculated against rabies and marked with a tattoo or microchip. Remember that not all accommodations allow for animals to stay in the rooms.

PHONE & MOBILE PHONE

The international code for calling Spain from abroad is +34, followed by the complete number. To call other countries, dial the country code (UK +44, US +1, Ireland +353), and then the telephone number without 0. Even for local calls in Spain, you must always dial the 9-digit number. The *Telefónica* phone boxes that are still in operation take coins and phone cards. Find out from your telephone provider what the fees and conditions are for calling and internet surfing abroad before going on holiday. Non-toll-free numbers in Spain start with 901 or 902; mobile numbers begin with a 6 or 7.

PHOTOGRAPHY

Memory cards and CDs cost more in Spain, while name-brand batteries are often cheaper to buy. Only in the museums are pictures not allowed to be taken.

WEATHER IN MÁLAGA

	Jan	Feb	March	April	May	June	July	Aug	Sept	Oct	Nov	Dec
Daytime temperatures in °C/°F	16/61	17/63	18/64	21/70	23/73	27/81	29/84	29/84	27/81	23/73	19/66	17/63
Nighttime temperatures in °C/°F	8/46	9/48	11/52	13/55	16/61	19/66	21/70	22/72	20/68	16/61	12/54	9/48
☀	6	6	6	8	10	11	11	11	9	7	6	5
☂	5	5	6	3	2	1	0	0	2	4	6	5
≈≈	15/59	14/57	14/57	15/59	17/63	18/64	21/70	22/72	21/70	19/66	17/63	16/61

POST

Post offices *(oficinas de correos)* are generally open *Mon–Fri 8.30am–2.30pm* and *Sat 9.30am–1pm*. Stamps can also be bought at the tobacconists *(estancos)*. If nothing has changed since this book was printed, a standard letter or postcard within Europe currently costs 1.25 cents. *www.correos.es*

PUBLIC TRANSPORT

The Spanish railway network is not very extensive. There is, however, a good high-speed rail link (AVE, ALVIA) between Madrid via Córdoba to Seville and from Madrid to Málaga. If you buy a *Renfe Spain Pass*, you'll have one month to travel anywhere in Spain four (195 euros) to ten (410 euros) times. The pass can be used in connection with the AVE, ALVIA and all local transport. For information and reservations, see *www.renfe.com.* Intercity buses also offer great connections and are a good alternative to taking the train. Ask the tourist information centre about the bus stations *(estación de autobuses)* in your area. Travelling by bus or train is ideal for travellers with a small budget.

TIPS

After the waiter brings you your change on a plate, you can leave some on the plate. 5% to 10% is fine. Taxi fares should be rounded up. In hotels, chambermaids/roomboys are given 1–2 euros.

WHERE TO STAY

Choose to stay in a simple guesthouse, *hostale* or fine five-star hotel. If you understand Spanish, you can look for a country or design hotel at e.g. *Rusticae* (*www.rusticae.es*). Get more tips on where to stay in the country (*turismo rural*) at *www.raar.es*. With the exception of a few hotels, breakfast is usually not included in the price. If you have to pay, it's cheaper and often even better to eat in a nearby restaurant or café anyway. NOTE: Some hotels don't calculate the added value tax (SP: IVA) in the total amount.

YOUTH HOSTELS

For information on the 20 youth hostels located in Andalucía, call *tel. 9 02 51 00 00* or go online at *www.inturjoven. com*.

The legacy of the Romans: Baelo Claudia near Bolonia

USEFUL PHRASES SPANISH

PRONUNCIATION

c	before 'e' and 'i' like 'th' in 'thin'
ch	as in English
g	before 'e' and 'i' like the 'ch' in Scottish 'loch'
gue, gui	like 'get', 'give'
que, qui	the 'u' is not spoken, i.e. 'ke', 'ki'
j	always like the 'ch' in Scottish 'loch'
ll	like 'lli' in 'million'; some speak it like 'y' in 'yet'
ñ	'nj'
z	like 'th' in 'thin'

IN BRIEF

Yes/No/Maybe	sí/no/quizás
Please/Thank you	por favor/gracias
Hello!/Goodbye!/See you!	¡Hola!/¡Adiós!/¡Hasta luego!
Good morning!/afternoon!/ evening!/night!	¡Buenos días!/¡Buenos días!/¡Buenas tardes!/¡Buenas noches!
Excuse me, please!	¡Perdona!/¡Perdone!
May I ...?/Pardon?	¿Puedo ...?/¿Cómo dice?
My name is ...	Me llamo ...
What's your name?	¿Cómo se llama usted?/¿Cómo te llamas?
I'm from ...	Soy de ...
I would like to .../Have you got ...?	Querría .../¿Tiene usted ...?
How much is ...?	¿Cuánto cuesta ...?
I (don't) like that	Esto (no) me gusta.
good/bad/broken/doesn't work	bien/mal/roto/no funciona
too much/much/little/all/nothing	demasiado/mucho/poco/todo/nada
Help!/Attention!/Caution!	¡Socorro!/¡Atención!/¡Cuidado!
ambulance/police/fire brigade	ambulancia/policía/bomberos
May I take a photo here?	¿Podría fotografiar aquí?

DATE & TIME

Monday/Tuesday/Wednesday	lunes/martes/miércoles
Thursday/Friday/Saturday	jueves/viernes/sábado
Sunday/working day/holiday	domingo/laborable/festivo
today/tomorrow/yesterday	hoy/mañana/ayer

¿Hablas español?

"Do you speak Spanish?" This guide will help you to say the basic words and phrases in Spanish

hour/minute/second/moment	hora/minuto/segundo/momento
day/night/week/month/year	día/noche/semana/mes/año
now/immediately/before/after	ahora/enseguida/antes/después
What time is it?	¿Qué hora es?
It's three o'clock/It's half past three	Son las tres/Son las tres y media
a quarter to four/a quarter past four	cuatro menos cuarto/ cuatro y cuarto

TRAVEL

open/closed/opening times	abierto/cerrado/horario
entrance / exit	entrada/acceso salida
departure/arrival	salida/llegada
toilets/ladies/gentlemen	aseos/señoras/caballeros
free/occupied	libre/ocupado
(not) drinking water	agua (no) potable
Where is ...?/Where are ...?	¿Dónde está ...? /¿Dónde están ...?
left/right	izquierda/derecha
straight ahead/back	recto/atrás
close/far	cerca/lejos
traffic lights/corner/crossing	semáforo/esquina/cruce
bus/tram/U-underground/	autobús/tranvía/metro/
taxi/cab	taxi
bus stop/cab stand	parada/parada de taxis
parking lot/parking garage	parking/garaje
street map/map	plano de la ciudad/mapa
train station/harbour/airport	estación/puerto/aeropuerto
ferry/quay	transbordador/muelle
schedule/ticket/supplement	horario/billete/suplemento
single/return	sencillo/ida y vuelta
train/track/platform	tren/vía/andén
delay/strike	retraso/huelga
I would like to rent ...	Querría ... alquilar
a car/a bicycle/a boat	un coche/una bicicleta/un barco
petrol/gas station	gasolinera
petrol/gas / diesel	gasolina/diesel
breakdown/repair shop	avería/taller

FOOD & DRINK

Could you please book a table for tonight for four?	Resérvenos, por favor, una mesa para cuatro personas para hoy por la noche.
on the terrace/by the window	en la terraza/junto a la ventana

The menu, please/	¡El menú, por favor!
Could I please have ...?	¿Podría traerme ... por favor?
bottle/carafe/glass	botella/jarra/vaso
knife/fork/spoon	cuchillo/tenedor/cuchara
salt/pepper/sugar	sal/pimienta/azúcar
vinegar/oil/milk/cream/lemon	vinagre/aceite/leche/limón
cold/too salty/not cooked	frío/demasiado salado/sin hacer
with/without ice/sparkling	con/sin hielo/gas
vegetarian/allergy	vegetariano/vegetariana/alergía
May I have the bill, please?	Querría pagar, por favor.
bill/receipt/tip	cuenta/recibo/propina

SHOPPING

pharmacy/chemist	farmacia/droguería
baker/market	panadería/mercado
butcher/fishmonger	carnicería/pescadería
shopping centre/department store	centro comercial/grandes almacenes
shop/supermarket/kiosk	tienda/supermercado/quiosco
100 grammes/1 kilo	cien gramos/un kilo
expensive/cheap/price/more/less	caro/barato/precio/más/menos
organically grown	de cultivo ecológico

ACCOMMODATION

I have booked a room	He reservado una habitación.
Do you have any ... left?	¿Tiene todavía ...?
single room/double room	habitación individual/habitación doble
breakfast/half board/	desayuno/media pensión/
full board (American plan)	pensión completa
at the front/seafront/garden view	hacia delante/hacia el mar/hacia el jardín
shower/sit-down bath	ducha/baño
balcony/terrace	balcón/terraza
key/room card	llave/tarjeta
luggage/suitcase/bag	equipaje/maleta/bolso
swimming pool/spa/sauna	piscina/spa/sauna
soap/toilet paper/nappy (diaper)	jabón/papel higiénico/pañal
cot/high chair/nappy changing	cuna/trona/cambiar los pañales
deposit	anticipo/caución

BANKS, MONEY & CREDIT CARDS

bank/ATM/	banco/cajero automático/
pin code	número secreto
cash/credit card	en efectivo/tarjeta de crédito
bill/coin/change	billete/moneda/cambio

HEALTH

doctor/dentist/paediatrician	médico/dentista/pediatra
hospital/emergency clinic	hospital/urgencias
fever/pain/inflamed/injured	fiebre/dolor/inflamado/herido
diarrhoea/nausea/sunburn	diarrea/náusea/quemadura de sol
plaster/bandage/ointment/cream	tirita/vendaje/pomada/crema
pain reliever/tablet/suppository	calmante/comprimido/supositorio

POST, TELECOMMUNICATIONS & MEDIA

stamp/letter/postcard	sello/carta/postal
I need a landline phone card/	Necesito una tarjeta telefónica/
I'm looking for a prepaid card for my mobile	Busco una tarjeta prepago para mi móvil
Where can I find internet access?	¿Dónde encuentro un acceso a internet?
dial/connection/engaged	marcar/conexión/ocupado
socket/adapter/charger	enchufe/adaptador/cargador
computer/battery/ rechargeable battery	ordenador/batería/ batería recargable
e-mail address/at sign (@)	(dirección de) correo electrónico/arroba
internet address (URL)	dirección de internet
internet connection/wifi	conexión a internet/wifi
e-mail/file/print	archivo/imprimir

LEISURE, SPORTS & BEACH

beach/sunshade/lounger	playa/sombrilla/tumbona
low tide/high tide/current	marea baja/marea alta/corriente

NUMBERS

0	cero	14	catorce
1	un, uno, una	15	quince
2	dos	16	dieciséis
3	tres	17	diecisiete
4	cuatro	18	dieciocho
5	cinco	19	diecinueve
6	seis	20	veinte
7	siete	100	cien, ciento
8	ocho	200	doscientos, doscientas
9	nueve	1000	mil
10	diez	2000	dos mil
11	once	10 000	diez mil
12	doce	1/2	medio
13	trece	1/4	un cuarto

ROAD ATLAS

The green line indicates the Tour 'Andalucía at a glance'
The blue line indicates the other Discovery Tours

All tours are also marked on the pull-out map

Exploring Andalucía

The map on the back cover shows how the area has been sub-divided

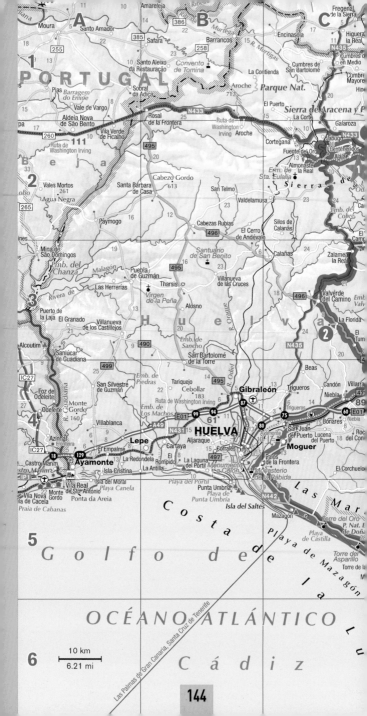

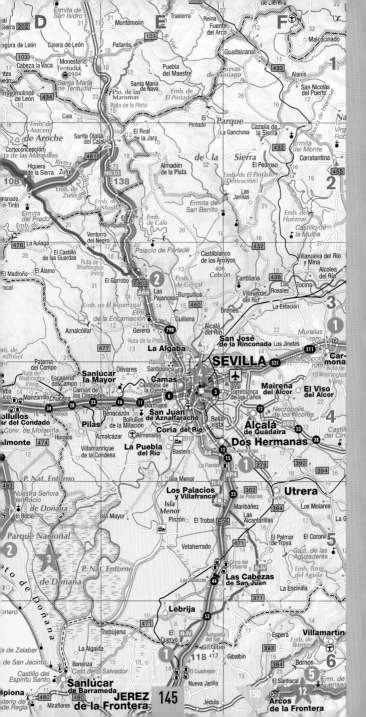

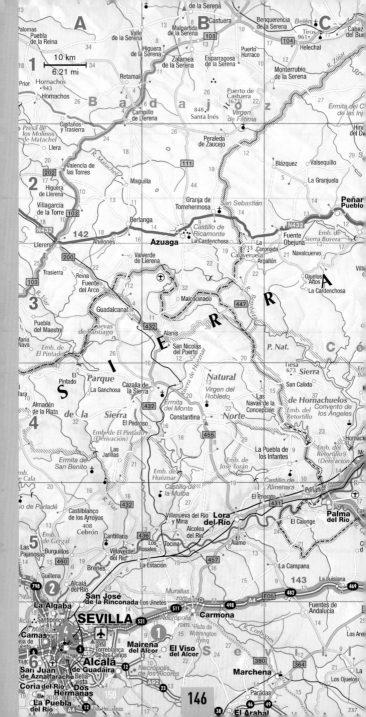

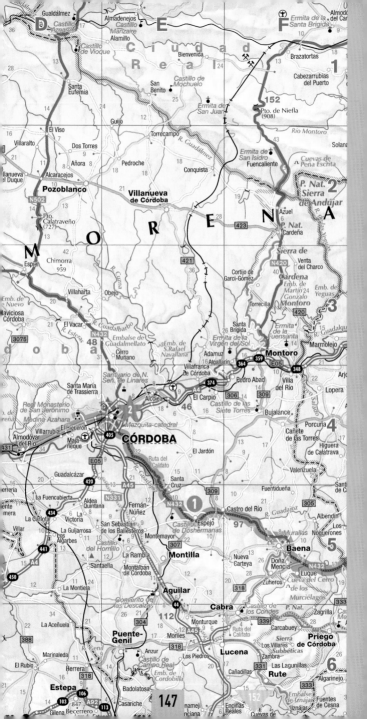

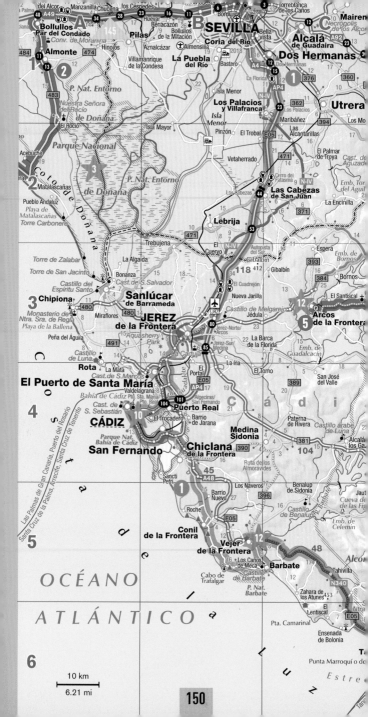

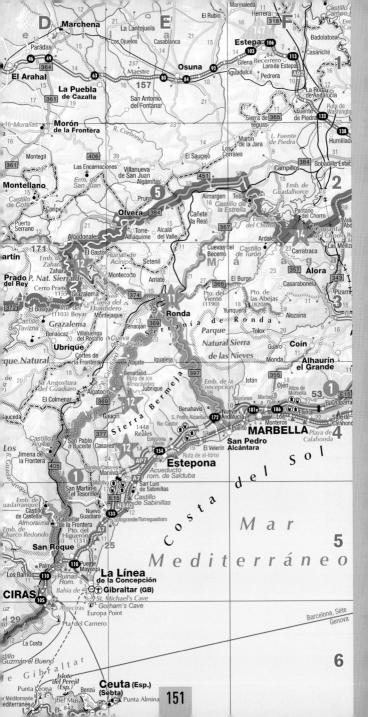

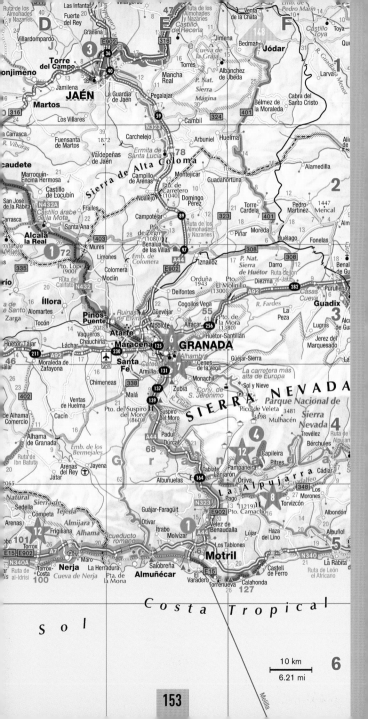

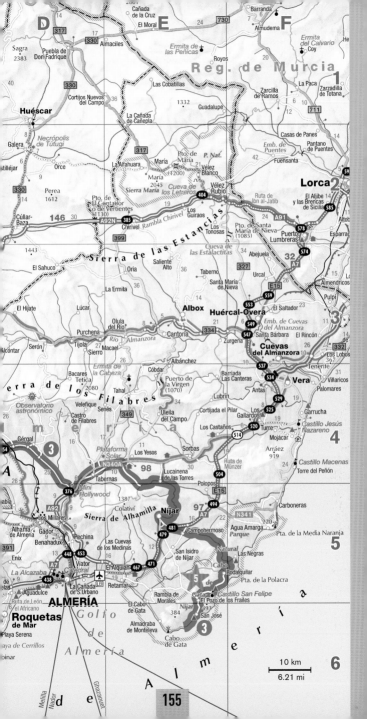

KEY TO ROAD ATLAS

Autobahn mit Anschlussstellen
Motorway with junctions

Autobahn in Bau
Motorway under construction

Mautstelle
Toll station

Raststätte mit Übernachtung
Roadside restaurant and hotel

Raststätte
Roadside restaurant

Tankstelle
Filling-station

Autobahnähnliche Schnell-
straße mit Anschlussstelle
Dual carriage-way with
motorway characteristics
with junction

Fernverkehrsstraße
Trunk road

Durchgangsstraße
Thoroughfare

Wichtige Hauptstraße
Important main road

Hauptstraße
Main road

Nebenstraße
Secondary road

Eisenbahn
Railway

Autozug-Terminal
Car-loading terminal

Zahnradbahn
Mountain railway

Kabinenschwebebahn
Aerial cableway

Eisenbahnfähre
Railway ferry

Autofähre
Car ferry

Schifffahrtslinie
Shipping route

Landschaftlich besonders
schöne Strecke
Route with
beautiful scenery

Alleenstr.   Touristenstraße
Tourist route

XI-V   Wintersperre
Closure in winter

× × × × ×   Straße für Kfz gesperrt
Road closed to motor traffic

8%   Bedeutende Steigungen
Important gradients

Für Wohnwagen nicht
empfehlenswert
Not recommended
for caravans

Für Wohnwagen gesperrt
Closed for caravans

Besonders schöner Ausblick
Important panoramic view

Wartenstein Sehenswert: Kultur - Natur
Umbalfälle Of interest: culture - nature

Badestrand
Bathing beach

Nationalpark, Naturpark
National park, nature park

Sperrgebiet
Prohibited area

Kirche
Church

Kloster
Monastery

Schloss, Burg
Palace, castle

Moschee
Mosque

Ruinen
Ruins

Leuchtturm
Lighthouse

Turm
Tower

Höhle
Cave

Ausgrabungsstätte
Archaeological excavation

Jugendherberge
Youth hostel

Allein stehendes Hotel
Isolated hotel

Berghütte
Refuge

Campingplatz
Camping site

Flughafen
Airport

Regionalflughafen
Regional airport

Flugplatz
Airfield

Staatsgrenze
National boundary

Verwaltungsgrenze
Administrative boundary

Grenzkontrollstelle
Check-point

Grenzkontrollstelle mit
Beschränkung
Check-point with
restrictions

ROMA Hauptstadt
Capital

VENEZIA Verwaltungssitz
Seat of the administration

MARCO POLO Erlebnistour 1
MARCO POLO Discovery Tour 1

MARCO POLO Erlebnistouren
MARCO POLO Discovery Tours

MARCO POLO Highlight
MARCO POLO Highlight

INDEX

This index lists all cantons, places, mountains and destinations featured in this guide. Numbers in bold indicate a main entry.

CREDITS

WRITE TO US

e-mail: info@marcopologuides.co.uk

Did you have a great holiday? Is there something on your mind? Whatever it is, let us know! Whether you want to praise, alert us to errors or give us a personal tip – MARCO POLO would be pleased to hear from you.
We do everything we can to provide the very latest information for your trip. Nevertheless, despite all of our authors' thorough research, errors can creep in. MARCO POLO does not accept any liability for this. Please contact us by e-mail or post.

MARCO POLO Travel Publishing Ltd
Pinewood, Chineham Business Park
Crockford Lane, Chineham
Basingstoke, Hampshire RG24 8AL
United Kingdom

PICTURE CREDITS

Cover Photograph: Segura de la Sierra in Sierra de Cazorla (Schapowalow/SIME: R. Spila)
Photos: DuMont Bildarchiv: Gonzales (130 bottom, 137); R. Gerth (60, 62/63); huber images: R. Schmidt (37); huber images/SIME: P. Canali (55), S. Mezzanotte (80), M. Rellini (93), S. Scattolin (38/39), A. Serrano (18 bottom), G. Simeone (103); huber images/SIME/4Corners: J. Wlodarczyk (32/33); huber images/SIME/4Corners;: S. Wasek (20/21); huber-images: C. Dutton (51), G. Gräfenhain (1427142), J. Lawrence (104/105); huber-images/SIME: J. Huber (12/13); © istockphoto.com: Alija (18 M.); M. Kirchgessner (123); laif: Gonzales (47); Laif: M. Gónzalez (57), M. Jäger (120/121), Tophoven (flap r.), L. Vallecillos (48/49), Zinn (41); mauritius images: R. Mattes (75); mauritius images/age (114); mauritius images/age fotostock: J. Alba (85), J. Antonio Moreno (43), J. Aparicio (4 bottom), A. Cano Miño (25), J. Carlos Muñoz (34, 82), M. Ramírez (128/129), G. Rooney (44); mauritius images/Alamy (2, 3, 4 top, 9, 19 top, 26/27, 28 r., 50, 66, 71, 111, 116, 130 top), J. Alba (90, 126), S. Black (14/15), E. Bombarelli (18 top), P. Bonbon (11), W. Doyle (5, 10, 89), P.v. Munster (17), L. Vallecillos (78), K. Welsh (124/125); mauritius images/Alamy/dbimages (19 bottom, 69); mauritius images/Alamy/FR Images (6); mauritius images/Axiom Photographic: B. Welsh (99); mauritius images/Chromorange: J. Feuerer (73); mauritius images/Hemis.fr: P. Escudero (23); mauritius images/Image Source: Z. Kendal (76/77); mauritius images/Imagebroker: B. Boensch (88); mauritius images/TPP: N. Lisovskaya (28 l.); mauritius images/Trigger Image (86); D. Renckhoff (7, 29, 30/31); Schapowalow/SIME: R. Spila (1); A. Selbach (8, 131); O. Stadler (58/59, 96/97); White Star: Gumm (30, 52, 65, 129); T. P. Widmann (flap l., 31, 94, 101, 128)

2nd edition – fully revised and updated 2019
Worldwide Distribution: Marco Polo Travel Publishing Ltd, Pinewood, Chineham Business Park, Crockford Lane, Basingstoke, Hampshire RG24 8AL, United Kingdom. Email: sales@marcopolouk.com
© MAIRDUMONT GmbH & Co. KG, Ostfildern
Chief editor: Marion Zorn
Author: Martin Dahms; Co-author: Lothar Schmidt; Editor: Nikolai Michaelis
Programme supervision: Lucas Forst-Gill, Susanne Heimburger, Johanna Jiranek, Nikolai Michaelis, Kristin Wittemann, Tim Wohlbold, Picture Editor: Gabriele Forst; What's hot: wunder media, Munich, Lothar Schmidt; Cartography road atlas/pull-out map: © MAIRDUMONT, Ostfildern; Design: Front cover, pull-out map cover, p. 1: Karl Anders – Büro für Visual Stories, Hamburg; Interior Design: milchhof:atelier, Berlin; Design p. 2,3, Discovery tours: Susan Chaaban Dipl.-Des. (FH)
Translated from German by Christopher Wynne and Rotkel Textwerkstatt, Berlin; editor of the English edition: Sarah Trenker and Rotkel Textwerkstatt, Berlin; Prepress: Rotkel Textwerkstatt, Berlin; Phrase book in cooperation with Ernst Klett Sprachen GmbH, Stuttgart, Editorial by Pons Wörterbücher

MIX
Paper from responsible sources
FSC
www.fsc.org   FSC® C124385

DOS & DON'TS

When in Andalucía do as the Andalucíans do

DINING OUT TOO EARLY

It's 8pm, and you head out to into the city to get a bite to eat. When you walk into the restaurant, however, you see there's not a single guest sitting at the tables. Have they not opened yet? Quite the contrary! You're just too early. Andalucians generally don't go out for dinner until 9pm. And it's even later in the big cities and during summer. Then they go out at 10pm, perhaps even at 11pm. It's uncommon for people to have lunch before 2pm/2.30pm, and they usually don't leave the restaurant until at least four or five.

SITTING WITH STRANGERS

The bar is packed. In the corner, you see some empty seats at a table with just one Spaniard sitting at it. But don't think about asking if you can join him at his table. No Andalucían would ever think of sitting down with someone they don't know!

SHOP DURING THE SIESTA

Are you making plans to casually stroll through the alleyways and do some afternoon shopping today? Forget about it! The small shops and boutiques gernerally stay closed between 1pm/2pm and 4.30pm/5pm.

CLAPPING TO THE MUSIC

Clapping together with the performers during a flamenco concert is just about on a par with singing with an opera singer during the performance. *Palmas*, the rhythmic clapping of hands, is an integral part of the music and only those who are experts clap. Only in the *Tablaos* for tourists do they make an unfortunate exception.

DON'T HELP PICKPOCKETS

Andalucia is not any more dangerous than other parts of Europe. But there are still thieves who lie in wait to steal. It's best you keep an eye on your valuables. Don't leave anything valuable in a parked car. Don't carry your papers in a handbag. Store them in a bumbag than, and in confusing or hectic situations, wear your rucksack in the front of you.

SPLITTING THE BILL

Don't overwhelm the waiter by asking them to split the bill. It's more common in Spain for one person to take the whole bill. Just agree on who will pay it next time. That way everything remains fair in the end.

DON'T ASSUME EVERYONE SPEAKS ENGLISH

The world is ours for the taking – well, that's what a lot of tourists think. They assume they can speak just like they do at home. English may be a global language, but how about asking in Spanish first? Just ask, *¿Habla inglés?* The Spanish are not the best linguists, and they appreciate it when foreigners try to speak a bit of their mother tongue.